Dedication

To GOD:

"WITH GOD ALL THINGS ARE POSSIBLE."
MATTHEW 19:26b

Contents

	Foreword by Rosey Grier vii
	Introduction ix
1.	The Mystery 13
2.	Awesome Miracles 19
3.	Growing Up 25
4.	Hellos and Good-Byes 33
5.	Yo-Yo Christianity 43
6.	You're in the Navy Now 49
7.	New Marching Orders 55
8.	Discovering God Again 63
9.	Love, Honor and Cherish 69
10.	The Route to Church 75
11.	The Lord is My Shepherd 81
12.	My Confusion, Not God's 91
13.	Regrets 99
14.	The First Big Ending 103
15.	After the Lunch Was Over 109
16.	The End for Now 117
	With Appreciation 125
	The Missionary Writing Team 127

Foreword

Penny Gillett is my all-time favorite lady. I met her at the 1993 National Veterans Wheelchair Games in San Antonio. A gentleman brought me a note which read, "I'm called to be a missionary, now what?" The man just stood there and looked at me. Then I said, "Who sent this?" He replied, "That lady over there in the wheelchair." I went over to her and she turned around to face me. After we had talked for about an hour, Penny's sister, Bonnie, lifted Penny's arms up and placed them around my neck so she could hug me. I bent down to receive her hug and to hug her back, but when I straightened up my heart stayed with her. Why were we crying? It was because I saw a depth in her that was so deep that only God Himself could answer. All around was joy and the love of the Lord.

I guess her book, **Miracles in the Darndest Ways**, is very apropos. Her book is so insightful and it touches so many nerves. She shares her struggles, her dreams and her accomplishments; all through the power of God. She talks about what it means to be a Christian, what it means to have doubts and what it means to have strong faith. Penny hasn't always had it easy. In fact, many would have given up if their name wasn't Penny Gillett Silvius. Certainly she has had her reasons to doubt, but God has come through for her each time, giving her strength and courage to go on. There's a statement Penny made that stays in my mind. "Although I will die with MS, I won't die from it." She has had multiple sclerosis (MS) for a lot of years, yet it has not stopped her. Over every valley, there has been a bridge; out of every pit, a ladder. And the one who has always given her a new beginning has God Himself, through friends, relatives and loved ones.

I think this is a marvelous book of courage. It shows that regardless of your circumstances, with the help of God and hard work, you can be the missionary, the doctor, the lawyer, the preacher, the teacher, or anything that God calls you to do because you're only limited by yourself. I congratulate Penny on writing this book on her life and I know that her testimony will move people to say, *"If she can do it, I can do it!"* **Miracles in the Darndest Ways... I love it!**

Love,

Rosey Grier

INTRODUCTION

MIRACLES

Miracles are happening all the time and all around us. I believe whenever a prayer is answered, a miracle has taken place. The problem is that we often don't acknowledge that our prayers have been answered. I see several reasons for this lack of acknowledgment. One reason could be that after praying or even not praying for something, we deny that a miracle has occurred. For example, when my husband goes on business trips, I pray that he will return home safely. When he comes home, I could say to myself, "What were the chances that he would have come home safely anyway? Maybe my prayer really made no difference. Maybe this wasn't a miracle." The truth is, whether I had prayed or not, God brought this man home safely. This is one of God's miracles. I am getting better at thanking God for these miracles when my prayers are answered.

Another situation where we do not give God His deserved credit for miracles is when, although we pray, we give someone else the credit. For example, when Dad was in the hospital, I prayed continually for his healing, that Jesus the Great Physician would intervene and restore his strength. When he was finally home and back to his near-normal self, I began to give the credit to the doctors. The credit, of course, belonged to the Great Physician, Jesus Christ, who led the doctors in helping to heal my father.

Another reason could be that we just aren't paying attention. Although we pray for something and our prayers are answered, we may not be thinking along the lines of cause and effect. We may not remember, "Oh, yeah, I prayed for that exact same thing." Do you believe in coincidences? Is it really a coincidence when you are thinking about someone and they come for an unexpected visit? Is it really a coincidence when you receive a bonus at the same time your car needs major repairs? I believe this is another example of God's miracles that we often miss. In Kelsey Grammar's book, So Far..., he refers to coincidences as "God's way of covering up His footprints." I like that. In other words, if God doesn't have His footprint in neon lights, we attribute the incidence to coincidence. I consider the book that you are now reading to be a miracle. That does not make it unusual since many books are miracles. As you read on, I hope you can see why I place this in the "miracle" category. Hopefully, you will even agree with me.

MY PURPOSE

Several years ago I attended the funeral of a dear friend. As I opened the bulletin there was a page that contained a prayer written by this friend. It touched me so much that I framed it and have it hanging on my wall. I would like to share it with you.

MY PRAYER

By Rev. Eric W. Johnson

I do not ask that crowds shall fill the temple
And men along the walls shall stand;
I only ask that as I give the message
Folks shall reach out and touch His nail-pierced hand.

I do not ask for earthly recognition
And fame to fill the footsteps I have trod;
I only ask that somewhere in the message
Folks shall behold the precious Lamb of God.

I do not ask for nods from great and mighty
Or gain we mortals soon must leave behind;
I only ask that ere the service closes
Men shall in Christ eternal riches find.

I do not ask as coming year advances
For plush retirement on some favored isle;
I only ask when earthly years are ended
That Christ shall bid me welcome with a smile.

I do not ask the size of heaven's mansion,
If room there be for all friends far and near;
I only trust that someone shall enfold me
And say, "You told of Christ and that is why I'm here."

    I relate to this prayer because I have the same hope that Reverend Johnson had. I pray that some day in heaven, someone will say to me, "I am here because I discovered Christ through something you wrote."

CHAPTER ONE

THE MYSTERY

As I look around, this is no ordinary bedroom. We designed it specifically to be functional with the remote chance that I might have to be spending time here. All too soon, that remoteness became a reality. Oh, the bed is comfortable, but it's such a pain. As I lie in bed, I look around my room at the decorations. I know that some people don't hang decorations on their walls, (my mother-in-law and sister-in-law tend to be two of those people). I, on the other hand, like my walls covered with items which are memorable to me for my own enjoyment. I'm not a great decorator or anything like that. I just do it for myself. It gives me a variety of things at which to look. Right now as I look around my bedroom, I have ten items hanging on the wall—oops, make that eleven. I forgot the wreath which is hanging on the wall behind me. As I lie on my back, I notice, of course, there are no decorations on my ceiling.

Actually, I do have a fan with lights hanging from it. The fan is turning most of the time. One way in summer for cooling, reversed in winter for circulation. It is interesting to watch the fan and try to distinguish the individual blades. At times, when I stare intently, I can make out some of the individual blades, but most of the time it is just a blur of turning. As I look at the blur on my ceiling, my mind goes back to what led up to my spending so much time in this bed.

REMOTENESS BECOMES REALITY

I was an active, vibrant nineteen-year-old woman in the fall of 1973. Don't get me wrong, I am still an active, vibrant woman, but in a different way. I was not sure what was happening to my body in 1973, but I was experiencing a lot of pain and what I considered to be strange symptoms. The following summer things became clearer in one sense but even more confusing in another. I was diagnosed as having multiple sclerosis.

THE HARD FACTS

If you have MS, you probably know more about it than you would like. If you do not know much about MS, don't feel alone because you are one of millions. I have even found many doctors who don't know much about it either. In fact, I have been in the position of training the doctors about MS. If you have this disease, you have probably done the same. There are many theories as to what the cause of MS may be, but nothing is certain. Unfortunately, at this time studies have not come up with a cure. MS is a progressive disease of the central nervous system which consists of the brain and spinal cord. This is a neurological disease rather than a disease of the muscles. In other words, we are not Jerry's Kids!

As a simple example of how MS works, imagine, if you will, a lamp. Now focus on the cord which runs from the lamp and plugs into the wall. The cord may be made of cloth or plastic or whatever. What is important is what's inside the cord. That's the nerve center that brings electricity to the lamp and makes it work. Now imagine that the outside insulation of your cord is frayed or in some places just does not exist. That's when we have trouble. This is similar to what happens with MS. The coating of the nerves, a fatty tissue called the myelin sheath, is destroyed. As with the electrical cord, this insulation of the nerves aids in the transmission of the message. Without the myelin sheath, we have trouble just like with our lamp. In a nutshell, the messages do not get from the brain to the muscles so that the muscles will work properly. Symptoms usually appear between the ages of twenty and forty, although I was nineteen when my symptoms began. With better diagnostic procedures, MS is being diagnosed at a younger age; I have heard of cases diagnosed as young as fifteen. Some of the symptoms of the disease include blurred vision, slurred speech, extreme fatigue, loss of coordination, numbness or a prickling feeling, loss of balance, loss of bladder or bowel control and partial or complete paralysis of any part of the body.

THE PAIN EXPERIENCE

Another symptom of MS which is often misunderstood is pain. When I was first diagnosed in 1974, my major symptom was pain. At that time, doctors insisted that research indicated pain was not a symptom of MS. More recent research has discovered some patients with MS do experience pain. I could have told them that long ago. Today, it remains the symptom with which I have the greatest experience.

The pain for most patients I have come in contact with varies from mild to severe and occurs intermittently or constantly. I have spoken to some MS patients who are fortunate in that they have experienced no pain. I can not imagine that, but I certainly know it happens since MS cases vary in significant ways.

THE DISEASE CYCLE

The process of MS runs in exacerbations and remissions. During times of exacerbations, the symptoms worsen or new symptoms arise. I had an attendant who had trouble pronouncing the word "exacerbations." She just seemed to get tongue tied when she was talking to my nurse about exacerbations I was having. She just referred to it as the "E" word. Now, after all of this confusion another word that can be used for worsening of symptoms is "attack." Another part of MS is remissions where symptoms get better or completely disappear.

The way I see it, there are different types of MS. Although this may not sound technical, I will put it in lay terms, the language I like and the language to which I hope you will also relate. Some people may have only one episode of MS symptoms and then never have another recurrence. In fact, these people may not even be diagnosed. Their symptoms may be so fleeting they don't even seek medical attention for them.

The type that fits the typical definition of MS is where you have attacks and remissions. Chronic, progressive MS, although not common, is another category. It is characterized by periods of severe symptoms with rare periods of remission - although you may be hard pressed to find the remissions.

GOOD TIMES/BAD TIMES

As I mentioned, the usual process of MS is exacerbations and remissions. This is what my disease was like for about ten years. I had my bad times and I had my good times. During the good times, you could not even tell anything was physically wrong with me although I was still in a lot of pain and on medication. The bad times could be very strange.

With little warning, my eyes would start jumping or I would have weakness in my legs and I would have to use a cane or even a wheelchair for awhile. About ten years after my initial symptoms, I discovered another type of MS, the type with one exacerbation after another. I would have small remissions, but they were nothing to write home about. The exacerbations were much more powerful. I kept going down, literally.

After several falls, I ended up in a wheelchair. I had been in a wheelchair before, but this time it was different. I had lost a lot of body strength. The wheelchair was to become a permanent fixture for me. When I was still ambulatory, I was able to finish college, become licensed and work as a marriage, family and child counselor. The wheelchair did not stop this work. As a therapist and a college instructor, I often worked with people who had disabilities. When I was confronted with questions like "You've accepted your MS, haven't you?" I felt uncomfortable. Sure, I try, but was I at the point of total acceptance?

I gained some new insight on this one Sunday as I listened to my pastor's sermon. He said, "Our faith is not in concrete, it will be tested by life." I heard what he was saying, but I also came to an awareness for myself. Acceptance of multiple sclerosis is not in concrete. It is a process that is tested with new situations all through life. As the pastor spoke about faith, I was listening to his words in a way that really affected my life. With every crisis or barrier I face, I must reaccept my situation and my life with multiple sclerosis. Each step or other physical barrier is another situation to reevaluate and reaccept my life. With each attitudinal barrier and each new symptom of my disease comes new challenges of acceptance. I can't say that I have accepted my life with multiple sclerosis since that acceptance is always being tested, but I strive to continually be in the process.

Just as the wheelchair did not stop me, I also did not stop when I lost the use of my right arm and then my left arm. Sure, it slowed me down, but I still had a small counseling practice. What stopped my counseling was the loss of my voice. A counselor definitely needs a means of communication and at that point I had none. Sign language was not an option because of the limited use of my hands.

I went to school for eight years to learn to counsel, but I counseled for only ten years. That hardly sounds cost effective, does it? Obviously, the purpose of my education was not to spend my life as a counselor. God had other plans for me. Maybe my schooling was to help me write this book. I don't know. I guess we will find out together.

CHAPTER TWO

AWESOME MIRACLES

As I lie in bed looking around my room, my eyes focus on a small silver frame to my right. The burgundy backing supports a white oval stone that used to be a pin. On each side of the stone are matching tear drop earrings. My father's cousin, Phyllis, retrieved these along with a note from my paternal grandmother's house after Grandma died. About ten years later, when I was older and could really appreciate this treasure, Phyllis gave it to me. The note explained that these had belonged to my great, great grandmother. She was born in 1818. As I lie back and look at my ceiling fan turning, I try to imagine what life was like during that time. I find this task baffling. The earliest date that I can possibly think of imagining is 1954.

REMEMBER 1954

If nothing of importance happened to you in your life during that year, chances are you don't remember it specifically. You may, however, remember the era. You may have been very young, or not even born at the time, so therefore you don't have anything to remember. You can get a distorted idea of this decade by watching reruns of such TV programs as: "Father Knows Best," "The Andy Griffith Show" or "I Love Lucy." In 1954 a loaf of bread cost 17 cents, a gallon of gas cost 22 cents and a gallon of milk cost 92 cents. You could buy a new car for $1,700 or even a new house for $10,250, but minimum wage was only 75 cents and the average annual income was $3,960.

MIRACLES IN THE DARNDEST WAYS

Dwight D. Eisenhower was President with Richard M. Nixon as his Vice-President. Joe DiMaggio married Marilyn Monroe. People who were born that year included actor-director Ron Howard, tennis champion Chris Everett, and my best friend Vicki.

THE SETTING

On the evening of Monday, May 17, 1954, Barbara and Giles went to bed expecting the birth of their second child at any time. The baby was already a day late. At 4:00 a.m., Barbara woke up in labor. Giles loaded Barbara into their light green Ford and drove three and a half blocks to the Sigourney Hospital, which was located on the downtown square.

Sigourney (SIG . er . nee) was a small town in 1954 with a population of 2,343. It remains small with a 1992 population of 2,111. This town in Iowa has lots of character. The Keokuk County Courthouse stands in the center of the downtown square. The Courthouse Park has many interesting attractions. On the northeast corner of the square is the most stunning fountain I have ever seen, the John Q. and Josie Lewis Memorial Fountain. There are only five like it in the United States. It was erected in 1940 in memory of their five-year-old daughter who died of scarlet fever in 1883. The fountain has three basins of varying heights and is operated electrically. There are several changes in the water formations which are especially impressive at night when the colored lights alternately illuminate them. If you are in the area, it would be well worth your time to stop and see it. Across the sidewalk from the fountain is a statue of a soldier that stands on a granite monument. The plaque reads : "In memory and honor of the Union Soldiers of the Civil War 1861-1865." One of the buildings on the square, the hospital, had previously been a hotel and would later become a laundromat.

AT THE HOSPITAL

At about 7:00 a.m. Barbara's baby was ready but the delivery room was not. The lady occupying the room had not yet finished delivering her baby. Therefore, Barbara had to remain in the labor room. Although those were the days before a husband was with his wife during delivery, Giles was there because he was a physician. Since it is not customary for physicians to practice on their own families, in case there are complications, his co-worker was the attending physician.

The doctors immediately discovered, upon the first sight of the baby's head, that this was one of those complications. The baby was being born veiled. This means that the membrane was still intact and that there was a chance that the baby could aspirate the membrane into its lungs. This is what happened, although the doctors immediately tried to remove the membrane. Neither doctor had ever seen a baby born this way. In fact, Giles, in his thirty-three years of practice and delivery of over 750 babies, never saw one again.

LORD, WE NEED YOU NOW

The baby girl was delivered, but not breathing. The doctors took the baby to the corner of the room and worked on her to try to get her to breathe. "Working on her" consisted of the doctor holding the baby's head in his hand with the body extending up his arm. This way he could move the baby up and down in a rocking motion which loosened the mucous in the baby's lungs. The doctors were then able to suction mucous from the baby's mouth with a bulb syringe. After twenty minutes of this attempt, the baby was still not breathing. The attending physician reluctantly suggested that they give up the process. Giles could not imagine this. He could not imagine telling his wife that their baby was dead. He kept working and praying. After ten minutes more, his efforts proved to be effective. I was officially in the world.

As for Mom during all of this, she was not aware of the severity of what was happening. Just as it was not common for fathers to be in the delivery room at that time, "natural childbirth" consisted of drugging the mother to the extent that she could not feel pain. This also left her oblivious to her surroundings.

After the nurses cleaned me up, they took me to Mom's room, where she was first able to see me and hold me. The first thing she did was to check my toes. Dad had told her I had ten toes, six on one foot and four on the other. Mom knew better but she still had to check.

About two hours after I was returned to my incubator in the nursery, the nurses noticed that I was turning blue. They called Giles who had left and gone to his office about two blocks away from the hospital. The next thing Barbara noticed was a ruckus in the hospital hallways. Being an old building, the corridors echoed as Giles ran into the nursery and yelled to the nurses requesting emergency equipment. Needless to say, I was again revived. At that point my dad put together a special incubator which was unavailable at that time. It contained Alanair, which was a detergent that made bubbles in the incubator and had the therapeutic effect of liquefying mucous.

After day one I was out of the woods. This was the first miracle in my life. There were many other miracles surrounding this event. They could have, and in most cases did, go unnoticed. Psalms 139:16 says,

"You saw me before I was born and scheduled each day of my life before I began to breathe. Every day was recorded in your Book!"

(Living Bible)

How amazing! God has always been with us even before we were born. He knows everything that is going to happen to us even before it happens. This verse says to me that God knew the breathing problems I was going to have at birth and what the outcome would be even before I was born. He also knew that I would have MS. Even though we have free will, God knew how I would use my MS to glorify Him.

As I reflect back, some questions come to mind. I asked my mother why I was not brain damaged by this lack of oxygen. She said she had not thought, until many years later, that it could even have been a possibility. When I asked my dad the same question, he responded, "I really don't know. You must have gotten enough oxygen somewhere."

Have you ever noticed how we sometimes refer to God in terms that are never used to signify God in the Bible? For instance, when my Dad said "somewhere" what he really meant was, "You got the oxygen as a miracle from God." We also use other terms like "somehow," "something" and, my all time favorite, "coincidentally." I am not saying that when we use these terms we are always referring to God, but this is often the case. The next time you find yourself using one of these terms, try asking yourself: "Do I really mean God?"

CHAPTER THREE

GROWING UP

As I lie in bed looking around my room, my eyes focus on the frame in the corner. It is a beautiful certificate of holy matrimony for my maternal great grandparents dated 1899. When my grandmother asked me if I would like this certificate, it was in very bad shape. Not only had it been rolled up and folded, but someone had pasted it on brown contact paper. I still jumped at the chance to have the certificate.

After I was able to get this certificate restored, it became a beautiful work of art. Dogwood branches and flowers encircle this certificate of holy matrimony. At the bottom of this piece is a circle of silver surrounding a picture of Isaac standing and holding a staff. To the left of the circle are segments of Genesis 24:63 and 67 which say,

> "And Isaac lifted up his eyes and saw, and behold the camels were coming. And Isaac took Rebecca, and she became his wife, and he loved her."

There are several other Bible verses also included.

The whole certificate brings me to the conclusion that marriages at that time began with the Lord. A marriage based on the Lord leads to a family based on the Lord. Early religious experiences can be crucial to the development of a child. I have often thanked the Lord for my parents for providing me with such an experience during my young years. Although there were times when I strayed from the Lord, I know He was always with me. I cherish my up-bringing in a Christian Church.

FAMILY

Often we do not notice God's miraculous blessings. Instead, we take them for granted.

I was blessed with an extended Christian family. Until I was fourteen-years-old, I had the good fortune of living within fifteen miles of both my Grandma Verla and my Grandma Opal, my maternal grandfather Homer, Uncle Dick, Aunt Jean, some great-aunts and great-uncles and cousins from numerous generations. For several years, some of my great-grandparents were still living and residing near us. My immediate family consists of my parents and my two sisters. Renee is six years younger than I. I am one and half years younger than Bonnie.

Since Bonnie and I are so close in age, we have shared a special camaraderie. Throughout school, we had many of the same friends. We are still very close even though she lives an hour and half away from me. This may not sound very far, but with our busy lives it sure seems like a long distance.

Bonnie and I are so close that anything that affects Bonnie's life affects me. Therefore I would assume most occurrences in my life would affect her. MS and other disabling conditions do not affect just one person's life. It affects the lives of the entire family. My family is no exception.

Bonnie has adapted to the changes in my condition. This is not necessarily due to her knowledge of my disease as much as to her awareness and caring for me and my needs. I often wonder what would have happened if I had been the healthy sister and Bonnie had been the one with MS. Could I have been as sensitive to her needs as she is to mine? Would I or could I have been as supportive to her as she is to me? It takes a special person to be able to give the loving care that Bonnie has given me. I pray that everyone with MS could have a support person like Bonnie.

After I'd had MS for about twelve years, Bonnie went with me to the annual meeting of the Multiple Sclerosis Society. She was listening intently and taking numerous notes. I couldn't believe the flipping of pages on the tablet as she wrote. What was she finding so interesting? It was all old hat to me. After the meeting she told me, "I never really knew what MS was." When I asked her what she thought was going on with me she said, "Twelve years ago our parents essentially told me, 'We love Penny. She is sick. She has MS. We love Penny.'" With that little information Bonnie had been and continues to be a tremendous support to me.

RELIGION AT HOME

Although we would read Bible verses at Sunday School and church when I was growing up, we did not read the Bible in our home. My maternal grandmother, Grandma Verla was a strong Christian woman. When I was a child she was the only person I ever actually saw sit down and read the Bible for no apparent reason.

I remember having Bible story books. We looked through them and at some point we must have read them or someone read them to us. Have you ever seen the Bible stories they have on video tape now? I think they are great but might limit the family interaction that books offer. This does not have to be the case if the family watches them together. I remember the last time we sat and watched one of these video tapes. My parents, niece, nephew and I were all there. My dad was just as intrigued as his grandchildren were about the video. I try to expose the little ones to the Lord whenever possible.

When I was a child, my family usually prayed three times a day, although we were not necessarily always together.

At mealtime, we prayed:

"God is great, God is good; and we thank Him for our food. Amen"

When the whole family gathered for special occasions, like Thanksgiving and Christmas, Uncle Dick, my mother's brother, usually said the blessing. His prayers were more spontaneous and more relevant to the situation than our daily prayers.

At bedtime we prayed:

*"Now I lay me down to sleep
I pray the Lord my soul to keep,
God keep me through the night
And wake me in the morning light.
Amen"*

Now Grandma Verla, on the other hand, would say different prayers when she was staying with us or when we were staying with her. We were sure her prayers were not memorized. Sometimes she would pray about us, the things we were doing and would even mention our names just as if God knew who we were. That was my first exposure to the fact that we have a personal God.

I now realize that Grandma Verla had not been just a Sunday Christian, just as God is not just a Sunday God. Grandma had been a 24/7 Christian. In other words, she had been a Christian 24 hours a day, 7 days a week. Like Grandma Verla, I now strive to be a 24/7 Christian to serve God who is a 24/7 Lord.

... AND AT CHURCH

Although I now notice in the Sigourney paper that there are seven Protestant churches, as I was growing up I was only aware of three. The three main Protestant churches were the Methodist, Presbyterian and Christian. My family attended the Christian church.

My dad would usually drop Bonnie and me off for Sunday school and then Mom and he would meet us for church. Occasionally, Mom and Dad would go to Sunday school, too. We had our regular seats on the west side of the sanctuary. My dad sang in the choir. He sat in the back row so he could sneak out and answer the church phone when it rang, since it was usually for him anyway. My mom recalls one frightful Sunday when my father was asleep in the choir loft. So was Uncle Dick, who was the choir director. He sat on the end opposite my dad so he could easily move to the front to direct the choir. My mom was a bit nervous as they were both swaying in their chairs while they slept through the sermon.

Bonnie and I attended Vacation Bible School (VBS) usually twice each summer. We would attend once at our own church and once at Grandma Opal's church in Delta, Iowa, eight miles away. Delta had a population of five hundred. Vacation Bible School was a big occasion and I loved it. I still have my certificates of attendance. Even later, with my MS, I tried to attend Vacation Bible School whenever possible, either as a teacher or a helper. Now my participation is a lot different than it was. I lie in bed hearing about VBS from the church newsletter and praying for the children in attendance and for the adults who are there to help them.

RITES OF PASSAGE

There were several rites of passage in my church. At about age twelve, we took classes to teach us more about the hard facts of Christianity and about the church. This is when I accepted the Lord as my savior, was baptized and became a member of the church.

I remember my baptism was a special day. We had a baptismal pool behind the pulpit area in our church. Several people from my class were baptized the same day. When the curtain opened, I was standing in the water with Rev. Fuller. I remember his words, "In the name of the Father, the Son and the Holy Ghost," at which point he put the handkerchief over my face and immersed me into the water. As I arose from the water, the curtains began to close and I remember feeling different. This was an exciting time for me and I was proud to become a member of the church. I would later have the pleasure of re-experiencing this membership pride, but in an even stronger way.

Another rite of passage, which I was thrilled about, was joining the junior choir. I loved to sing and did so loudly as I praised the Lord. Fortunately, the only qualification to be in the choir was to be the proper age. I am told now that I can not carry a tune and I'm sure that I couldn't then either. However, I was proud to put on my red choir robe and sing with the junior choir when they appeared in the church. I now have a button that would have fit the situation. It reads, "Make someone happy. Keep quiet."

GROWING UP CHRISTIAN

As I look back on my childhood, I see the importance of my Christian upbringing. I think it is very important for every child to know of the Lord at a young age. Deuteronomy 6:5-7 states:

> *"Love the Lord your God with all your heart and with all your soul and with all your strength. The commandments that I give you today are to be upon your hearts. Impress them on your children. Talk about them when you sit at home and when you walk along the road, when you lie down and when you get up."*
>
> *(NIV)*

    They can always make a decision whether to follow the Lord or not later in life. A Christian background gives them a firm basis on which to make that decision.

    This is what I found in my life. Even though I strayed from the Lord more often than I care to remember, I could always return to Him. If I had not had that Christian upbringing I would not have had anything to go back to. Without this background, I would still be straying, especially when times got rough with MS and life in general.

    I thank my parents and grandparents for this gift of a foundation in Christ. Christian examples my grandparents had taught and modeled surfaced years later. They planted the initial seeds and watered them with their many prayers. Fortunately, I had other people planting seeds and watering them too. I know that Grandma Opal, my only surviving grandparent, still remembers me in her daily prayers. I also thank the Lord for giving me a fine Christian family.

CHAPTER FOUR

HELLOS AND GOOD-BYES

As I lie in my bed, looking around the room, I see several souvenirs that remind me of different places from my travels. On the wall next to the door there is a green, purple and gold Mardi Gras mask. I obtained this while visiting New Orleans. Next to it hangs a fuschia-colored silk flower lei. No, it is not from Hawaii, but from a Polynesian hotel we stayed at while visiting Disney World in Orlando, Florida. Even my furniture reminds me of several trips that my husband and I took to Amana, Iowa. Amana is located forty-five miles from my home town of Sigourney. Our furniture was crafted there by the famous Amish woodcrafters. As I lie back, my eyes focusing on the ceiling fan, I recall numerous trips to the Amana colonies. Many spontaneous excursions occurred when I was young. Other meaningful trips occurred later.

WHY MOVE?

When I was fourteen years old, my family moved to Kingsburg, California. My parents had lived in Sigourney for fifteen years, which was within twenty-five miles from the towns where they were born and raised. In other words, they weren't exactly nomads. But now, when I was thirteen years old, my parents started planning to move to Kingsburg, California, two thousand miles away.

My parents consulted my sisters and me on how we felt about moving. I wonder what would have happened if one or all of us had not wanted to move. Would they have actually changed their plans? Would we still be in Sigourney? It really doesn't matter because this move was God's plan for us. We all thought the move would be exciting at that time, but my circumstances changed in the year prior to the move. For one thing, I fell in love—but that is a later story.

CONDITIONS REQUIRED

My sisters and I had two conditions before we would move to California. The first condition was that we each have our own bedroom. That meant a four-bedroom house. Another condition that needed to be met was that we have a swimming pool because, being from Iowa, we believed everyone in California had a pool in their backyard. It is becoming more true now, but it certainly was not in the late sixties. In the three days that my parents were visiting Kingsburg, they bought the specified house and made all the arrangements to have the swimming pool built. Dad even had time to make arrangements for his new employment.

GOOD-BYE BEST FRIEND

Friends are blessings. Most of us are fortunate if we have one or two best friend experiences in our lives. My sister Bonnie and I both consider each other to be one of our best friends.

When I was two months old, we moved next door to Vicki. She was two months older than I. I can't remember a time when Vicki and I were not best friends. There were times when we had childhood spats, of course, but we always made up. Vicki attended the Presbyterian church and I attended the Christian church. Although they were two of the three main Protestant churches in town, they were the farthest apart. I mean this literally. Although the Christian church and the

Methodist were less than a block apart, the Presbyterian church must have been close to five blocks away. In addition to the physical distance, as a child I perceived the Presbyterian church to be different from the one I attended. This could have been perpetuated by the physical distance. The Methodist and Christian churches would have Vacation Bible School together but the Presbyterian church was too far away to be included.

With age came wisdom for me and I now realize how similar all three of these denominations are in doctrine. People can have religious differences and still be friends. Vicki and I are a prime example of this. We had what I perceived to be religious distance and we were still friends—in fact, we still are.

When we were in kindergarten, my family moved to a house about a mile from town. This was a major separation for children the age of Vicki and me. We kept our parents busy driving us back and forth to visit each other. Now, after this big move, she was in Iowa and I was in California. I never felt as close to friends in Kingsburg as I did to Vicki. Perhaps the absence of early growing up experiences prevented the kind of bonding I wanted. I had good friends in Kingsburg, but not like those in Iowa, or, more specifically, like Vicki. I even remember wishing the states between California and Iowa could be cut out. Then at least Vicki would be in the next state.

Unfortunately, people with MS, and, I am sure, people with other diseases and disabilities, sometimes lose friends because of their disabling conditions. Actually, it is the problem of the former friend who is able-bodied and not due to the disability itself. Unfortunately, that knowledge does not make it any easier when good friends leave. For example, when a person is first diagnosed with MS, their friends may not know how to treat them or what to say to them. I have noticed at different stages of my disability, friends have come and gone for different reasons. It did not make much difference when I started using a wheelchair, since at that time I became even more active and had a tendency to put people at ease. I noticed a few people shying away from me when I had difficulty grasping eating utensils. Okay, this attribute may not have made me the most elegant eating companion. Of course, it may not be surprising that when I became unable to "do lunch", I lost touch with a lot of people. In our society, much of our socializing centers around the eating process.

Although Vicki and I remain two thousand miles apart, we still keep in touch with letters and telephone calls. I had visited her many times in the first twenty-two years after I moved. Although we don't talk much about my MS directly, I have always felt her acceptance. I am sure Vicki loves and cares about me the same as before, the same as I feel about her. She recently confirmed this with a card she sent to me which illustrates the best friend concept. It tells of a best friend being there for advice, pep talks, or a shoulder to cry on. They know your secrets, fears and never stop believing in you. She went on to say I was that kind of friend to her and she was glad God brought me into her life. She called me her best friend, her forever friend.

GOODBYE FIRST LOVE

Not only was Vicki left behind, but my first love also lived in Iowa. Denny and I tried to hold onto each other, but two thousand miles was just too much to overcome. Each of us attempted to stay together, but not always at the same time. On my first trip back to Iowa to visit my grandparents I, of course, saw Denny. I was now a California Girl. I thought and acted like I was too cool. However, this had the effect of driving us farther apart.

The summer of 1969 was the next time I visited Iowa and saw Denny. Denny rode a motorcycle. My mother had never allowed me to ride with him. She considered it to be dangerous. When we were still very close, he told me he did not give rides to other girls. The one exception was one girl who he knew was a good friend of mine. He figured I wouldn't mind if he gave her a ride. I didn't at the time, but I surely did later. It was during my 1969 visit that I found out he was dating this former girlfriend of mine. This had the effect of making me very jealous. By this time, I realized I was not too cool and wanted Denny back.

As it turned out, Denny had the last word. On Thursday morning, September 11, 1969, just one year and three months after I had moved to California, my first love was tragically killed in a car accident. How do you deal with death, especially the death of someone you love?

GRIEVING

According to the psychologist, Elizabeth Kubler-Ross, who did extensive studies on death and dying, there are five stages of the grieving process. The five stages are: denial, anger, bargaining, depression and, finally, acceptance. People go through these experiences at different rates. Some people don't even experience all of these stages, or they may get stuck in one stage. They may also go through another stage so quickly that it is not noticeable. Some people may go back and forth from denial to anger and back to denial, or some may be going towards the acceptance stage and then backslide to anger or depression.

In my family, we tended to experience the denial stage quite heavily. I learned that stage of the process well. My father, being a doctor and the county coroner when we lived in Iowa, could not afford to treat death in an emotional way. He treated it in totally medical terms. In contrast, my mother would become physically ill so as to avoid funerals—the epitome of denial.

At the time of Denny's death, I did not have healthy grieving skills. In fact, I did not have these skills until I was half way through college. For more than ten years the Lord and I sporadically went through the process of grieving Denny's death.

GRIEVING MS

Grieving does not only occur following a death. The grief reaction is associated with any loss. It may be the loss of a job, the loss of a marriage, the loss of your belongings through a fire or a theft or the loss of your health.

When my cat, who I was extremely close to, died, I was devastated—even as an adult. I found strength where I didn't expect it and where I hadn't looked for it before. A phone call to Grandma Opal brought comfort and understanding. I was able to talk to her openly about death which filled a gap for me. We all have to have someone to talk to, especially during emotional times.

With MS there are many losses, but the grieving process may be a little touchy. For example, say a person with MS is grieving over their inability to walk without the assistance of a cane. Before they reach the acceptance stage their MS goes into remission. Yea!! The problem is that in three months, when they must use the cane again, the grieving process starts all over from the beginning. In some cases MS can become a perpetual grieving process. Although one aspect of the MS may be fully accepted, all too often there is something new that is popping up that must be dealt with using the grieving process.

We talked about death, but have you ever thought about your own death? Some believe that you must accept the fact of your own death before you can accept the death of others. Obviously, none of us will get out of this world alive, except for those who are taken with Christ at His second coming.

Some people think it is morbid to plan your own funeral. I have had people give me a hard time about me planning my funeral. It started when the doctor asked me about my wishes concerning life support equipment. My response to him was, "No, yes, I mean no, I mean I'm not quite sure." I wonder why my doctors sometimes refer to me as indecisive? What I needed to do was to talk to my pastor to make sure that what I wanted was consistent with what God wants. He assured me that whichever way I chose would be fine with God. My personal choice, and my husband agreed, was that I would not want heroic means of life support.

But why should death be a factor with my illness? MS is considered to be a chronic rather than a terminal illness. Supposedly it does not significantly reduce the person's life span. Although you will die with MS, you will not die from it. In some severe cases, MS leads to complications which in turn may result in death. That's like saying, when a person falls from a twenty story building, it is not the fall that kills them, it is the result of the landing. Either way you are dead. Some of the complications of MS include, but are not limited to: respiratory failure, choking, infections, malnutrition and pneumonia. Some people consider another possible side effect of MS that leads to death to be suicide. I contend that suicide has nothing to do with MS. Some people who have MS choose this method as a way out. That still does not mean that they are committing suicide because of MS. If they did not have MS they may have found another excuse to choose that route anyway. It is more likely that suicide is the result of an emotional disability.

REMEDY FOR GRIEF

In my counseling work, the grieving process was a frequent issue. Even if the death of a loved one had occurred many years before, it was often important to reach some sort of closure. That is not to say the goal would be to forget the loved one or hold them in lesser esteem, but just to reach closure in the grieving process.

One effective step I have found in the grieving process is to write a letter to the deceased person. Although I speak of the loved one and the person this could even be someone you didn't know too well but still held in high admiration. Or, it could certainly be a pet. Pets are often held in higher esteem than many people.

A letter can express feelings of love, confusion or anger. Although people are often reluctant to admit they are angry at someone who is dead, this is a very common feeling. They may be experiencing unexpressed, pent up anger from the past or anger at their loved one for leaving them. Yes, even though the loved one did not have control over their death and therefore is not realistically to blame, we still may be angry at them for leaving. Our feelings are not always rational, especially in highly emotional times. It is important we recognize these feelings, whether rational or not.

When my grandfather died a few years back, I was unable to physically write and was uncomfortable dictating the letter, although I wrote it several times in my mind. What I did dictate was the following poem about writing the letter, which helped me in saying good-bye to my Grandpa.

PENNY GILLETT SILVIUS

Letter to Grandpa

The other day I wrote a letter to my Grandpa.
I told him I wish we could see each other.
I told him I miss our talks
(Grandpas always have good stories to tell)
I told him how I enjoyed our fishing trips.
I caught the fish and he baited the hook.
The fish were small, but there were a lot of them.
They sure made for good eating!
I told him how I liked our car rides.
Grandpa knew every road in the county.
He had lived in the county all his life
and had been on the Board of Supervisors.
I told him that I miss him and that I love him.
When I finished the letter I didn't know where to send it.
I folded the pages, turned it over and wrote
"Grandpa, Heaven".
Then I placed it in my Bible;
I'm sure he got my message.

In Memory of Homer Rohloff 1901-1992

CHAPTER FIVE

YO-YO CHRISTIANITY

As I lie in bed looking around my room, I focus on a frame above my left shoulder. It is a simple wooden frame with a small gold border around the inside. The frame is nothing special, but what it contains is. I got the frame to hold the calligraphied lyrics to the song, "Because He Lives," that my girlfriend made for me. One day I would like to get the "Because He Lives" song lyrics nicely framed. Meanwhile, this simple frame supports a buff colored paper with small red flowers in the upper corners and the beautiful song lyrics to "Because He Lives." The chorus is especially meaningful as it reads:

> "Because He lives I can face tomorrow,
> Because He lives all fear is gone,
> Because I know He holds the future
> and life is worth the living just
> Because He lives."
> By William J. and Gloria Gaither

As I lie back looking at my rotating ceiling fan I think how fortunate I am to be back with the Lord and to know that He lives.

FOUNDATION OF FAITH

As I mentioned before, I had a strong Christian upbringing up to the age of thirteen. Reverend Kirby Fuller was the first minister that I remember in my life. Reverend Fuller helped me in establishing a religious foundation. He led classes on Christianity that I attended when I was about twelve years old. The teachings were not intense, but were appropriate to my age. The extent of my commitment was also in direct relation to my understanding.

TOMMY SMOTHERS

I would like to use the Yo-Yo Man, Tommy Smothers, to help explain the yo-yo Christianity concept which illustrates my Christian life. Tommy Smothers is part of the Smothers Brothers comedy team, along with his brother Dick. They were especially popular in the 1960's when they had the Smothers Brothers Comedy Hour which I understand was politically controversial. Since Tommy does not do yo-yoing in professional competition, he doesn't have an official title. As a lay person I would give him the lay title of "Yo-Yoist Extraordinaire." He even has a video tape demonstrating his yo-yo expertise.

When Tommy is holding the yo-yo in his hand before performing his tricks, I equate this with my being in God's hands. I was definitely in the hands of God in my childhood.

As Tommy opens his hand and releases his yo-yo to begin tricks, it is at this time that the yo-yo is farthest from Tommy's hand. I can easily equate this with the times of my life when I was doing my own thing, and not living with God. I believe during Tommy's yo-yo tricks, there are times when the yo-yo returns to Tommy's hand for a brief time. Similarly, even when I was doing my own thing there were times when I would return to God's hands. Unfortunately, these times were much too fleeting as I did not stay with God. Just as Tommy never lost control of his yo-yo because of the attached string, the Lord never let me go because I was attached to Him.

At the end of Tommy's yo-yoing, the yo-yo is again securely in his hand, just as it was before he began doing his tricks. I will even go out on a limb and speculate that Tommy is holding his yo-yo tighter at this point - even tighter than he held it initially. That's how it is with God and me. I'm securely in God's hands now. This time, I'm here to stay.

HOME WITHOUT A CHURCH

By California standards, Kingsburg was a small town with a population of about thirty five hundred. The area also supported approximately thirty churches. Although we attended several churches, we never felt like one was our home. Not only did we not feel welcome, one preacher even suggested we would be happier if we found another church. This advice followed the preacher discovering that my parents had vacationed in Las Vegas, although they certainly had not tried to keep it a secret. Apparently, this was not acceptable to him and to some other churches due to their interpretations of the Bible and what God wants from us. Personally, I could not figure out what the big deal was about Las Vegas. My parents, our pastor from Iowa and his wife went to Las Vegas together on several occasions. In fact, they still do. I guess it has to do with your attitude and reasons for going. My parents went strictly for entertainment. They were not taking anything away from the family or the church.

Of course, we did not attend all the churches in Kingsburg and obviously did not attend enough of them. The aforementioned experience may have caused us to be reluctant to search much further. We became a family without a church in California. I don't think we realized the impact this situation would have on our lives.

THE SEARCH GOES ON

My involvement with church and with the Lord primarily revolved around boys. Sometimes I would go to a boy's church with him. This often included the Catholic church, which was very unfamiliar to me. I was cool, however, and just followed what my date was doing.

I was deeply involved with the International Order of Rainbow for Girls which I dearly loved. Much of the ritualistic work was biblically based. As we repeated memorized words meeting after meeting, it became rote and took on minimal religious tones. Religion was not a regular part of our meetings or activities. For us, socializing and service projects were more important.

For a short time I was involved with Young Life. It attempted to introduce the concept that religion for young people could actually be fun. Our meetings were usually followed by a short devotional. Young Life met in our home a few times before they had their own meeting place. My most vivid memory of this group was when one of the leaders swallowed a live goldfish. This was a crowd pleasing gimmick for a short while during those days.

I was also involved with "The Lighthouse" for a short time. This was a Christian coffee house that was popular during the late sixties and early seventies. I remember the booths and psychedelic decorations created an atmosphere that was dim and mellow. The booths in the front were used for people to openly share the Word. A beaded doorway led to other rooms for individualized prayer and acceptance of or rededication to the Lord. I considered "The Lighthouse" radical by my standards and did not go there for very long.

TEEN ANGEL?

I was sincere about my convictions to the Lord during my involvement with Christian activities. I wish I could say that I always felt a connection with the Lord, but there was a time, unfortunately, when I became agnostic. I rebelled against everything, and this included God. I took nothing by faith and wanted everything to be proven to me. I had lost my trust in God. I went back and forth, in and out of my Christianity while I was in my twenties. I was almost thirty years old when I ended up securely in God's hands. This was due to, or possibly in spite of, my MS; but, most importantly, this time it was for good. All I had to do was open my eyes. God's wonderful creations have always been around me. Bouquets of flowers blooming in the springtime, the warm sunshine streaking into a beautiful orange, yellow and red glow as it sets at twilight, the stars sparkling through the darkness: all of these blessings and many more He has freely given us. God's miracles are unmistakable. They are manifested all around us. These are all proof of God's existence and of His love.

CHAPTER SIX

YOU'RE IN THE NAVY NOW

As I lie in bed looking around my room, my attention is drawn, momentarily, to my wheelchair. I then focus on the backpack that is hanging on my chair. There are over fifty pins attached to my pack. Many are from places I have visited. A lot of these places I went to for the National Veterans Wheelchair Games. Some of the pins are the same. About a dozen of them are of the American flag or contain the American flag. I have always been patriotic. I really don't know why. Maybe I inherited it from my father. Dad would fly the flag even when it wasn't Flag Day. As a matter of fact, I do the same today. My flag is flying most of the time.

- *GOD BLESS AMERICA*

In high school, I remember someone wrote an article for the school newspaper, The Viking Voice. She spoke against the flag and opposed the flag salute. In the next issue of The Viking Voice I had my rebuttal article where I stated I was proud to be an American and was proud to have the privilege to salute the flag of my country. I wish I had that article today. I think it was good, at least for a junior in high school.

When guys did not know what to do after they graduated from high school, I would suggest they go into the service. They would respond, "That's easy for you to say because you're not the one that's going." I fooled them. I was the one who went. Most of them did not. My parents were not opposed to my joining the Navy. In fact, they wanted someone to look after me. They figured Uncle Sam was as good as anyone. Little did they know.

WHAT A LIFE

Going into the Navy was also a way for me to demonstrate my independence, which of course, is important for teenagers. I was finally on my own. That is, after boot camp. I made good money, or so I thought. The Navy provided food, a place to stay and strange clothing. I was proud to be in uniform. They paid for my schooling while I was training for my job as a hospital corpsman. At the time, my goal was to become a nurse and I was hoping to be sent to nurse's training while in the Navy. That sounded like a good deal to me.

I loved the Navy. I could walk down the street on base and have something in common with everyone I met. First of all, we were all in the Navy. We also wore similar clothes or had them in our lockers back at the barracks. I was a 4.0 sailor. In Navy terms, that's like an "A" student. I even looked Navy - so much so that they used me for a Naval recruitment advertisement in a magazine. Actually, they chose three other people and myself. I was the only woman in the advertisement. They also flew in a typical high school guidance counselor from Orlando, Florida. I'm not sure what they were thinking of because he certainly didn't look like any high school counselors I knew. They paid my colleagues and me one dollar for posing and for the release of the picture. I wonder what they paid the guidance counselor. A friend of my mother's just happened to see the advertisement in a Teacher's Scholastic Magazine. She recognized me not only because I resemble my mother but because my name tag was visible. We had taken several serious pictures and several fooling around. The two-page advertisement in this magazine was one of the fooling around pictures.

HOSPITAL DAZE

I joined the Navy on March 16, 1973, to work in the hospital. Eight months later I was a patient with unexplainable back pain. As I dictated, read, edited and re-read the following section, I found it to be increasingly confusing. After thinking long and hard about this, the confusion spiraled. Not only did the hospital daze confuse me as I think about them now, but I realize I was baffled by them over twenty years ago as they were occurring.

I still feel it's important to include this information. I must warn you, if you begin feeling a bit puzzled it is completely unavoidable and actually to your advantage. At the point of your confusion you are struggling with the same feelings I was encountering.

Apparently I had a slight urinary tract infection which the pain was initially attributed to. Well, the infection cleared up. So why was I still experiencing pain?

The testing continued. One memorable event was when I got an injection in my back. I understood it to be a nerve block. A couple of hours later several doctors and nurses came into the room. They helped me out of bed. My legs were like putty and I started to sink to the floor. The medical staff caught me and put me back into bed. Without explanation, everyone left the room. I was scared to death. I didn't know what was happening. Were my legs going to start working again? I was 19 years old. I had been raised by a doctor and learned well from him. But not all of what I learned was accurate. One inaccurate thing I learned was that doctors always knew what they were doing. This led to my belief that I do not ask questions. Being a good patient, I dutifully conceded to whatever they said or did not say.

I never asked what was happening when my legs turned to putty. I do not know if they discovered anything or not. I did not even know what they were trying to accomplish. I just assumed it had something to do with the process of fixing me. I guess, due to my passive behavior at that time, I will always have questions in my mind. "What were they doing? What were they trying to do?" Years later, I discovered the doctors did not know it all. I assumed the doctors would tell me what I needed to know, so I would not ask questions. I was in my twenties before I heard my father say the words, "I don't know." I was amazed because I assumed he knew everything.

My husband went to the doctor with me when I was in my early thirties and he was shocked to find how passive I was with the medical staff. I sat like a meek child assuming the doctors knew my condition and the symptoms associated with it. I did not even give them much information about what was happening to me physically. Of course, being the good patient I was, I didn't ask questions. It took a lot of hard work to overcome this passivity. Today, I struggle to be assertive with the doctors. Now I strive to tell them exactly what I want and need. I find that, at times, I need to train them about my condition in general. This is especially important with MS since each case is different. I also find that, at times, they are not happy to see me coming.

Well, my legs did start working shortly after the injection and even the pain in my back got better. Although the cause of the pain was not determined at that time, I was released from the hospital, put back on active duty, but assigned to a desk job.

HOSPITAL DAZE AGAIN

I carried on really well for about four months. Then it started again, just like before with the back pain. So back to patient status in the hospital I went. I was in pelvic traction most of the time. What the traction seemed to accomplish was to constantly pull me to the foot of the bed.

When they finally gave up on the traction I was able to walk down the hallway. I glanced into a room where a woman was in a circular bed and she had pins in her head. The bed had to be turned periodically, which was an amazing sight. This woman was not in the military herself, but her husband of a few short weeks was in the Navy. They had been in an automobile accident. She broke her neck but he came out of it fine.

MY ROOMIE

I later became roommates with Fran after the pins were removed from her head. Neither Fran nor I had many visitors and we became good friends. Fran was a strong Christian lady and she influenced me in my faith at that time. We read the Bible together and prayed, mainly for healing. Our prayers were basically out of our discomfort and discontent, at least it was my discontent. I knew that God could heal. The Bible said He wanted to heal, so why didn't He get a move on and do it? Romans 5:3 states,

> "We can rejoice too, when we run into problems and trials for we know that they are good for us. They help us learn to be patient."
>
> *(Living Bible)*

I obviously had not learned patience yet. Sometimes I felt like my prayers were going no further than the ceiling.

Fran left the hospital before I did. I saw her about three years later braceless and very healthy. Apparently her prayers had gone a little further than mine because she had been healed. God can and does heal. I knew that.

I definitely believe in God. In fact, I found myself feeling angry at Him. What was so terrible about me that He did not heal me? He proved that he could heal because Fran's prayers had been answered. She was healed. What was it about her that made her better than me? What made us so different as people that she should receive healing and I did not? Sure, at that time I was not walking with the Lord, but I had tried. I also found myself feeling a bit jealous of Fran because she had been healed. With that came guilt for not being happy with my friend's good fortune.

YOU'RE OUT OF HERE

In May of 1974, only one year and two months after I had gone into the Navy, I was sent home awaiting orders. I was 35 pounds lighter than when I went into the hospital, which left me at 95 pounds. I was equipped with braces to support my back and feeling pretty miserable. My faith had dwindled by this time and I was mad at God. My orders came two months later. They were an honorable discharge for medical reasons which were stated as. . . "chronic low back pain with psychophysiologic musculoskeletal reaction." Now, what does this really mean? I had no idea.

CHAPTER SEVEN

NEW MARCHING ORDERS

As I lie in bed looking up, I am glad we chose to put in coffer ceilings. It makes for a unique view. When my husband and I were making plans to build a house, we looked at many houses both new and old. One thing I observed that I really liked was the coffer ceilings. Although I had probably seen them many times, I had not been aware of them before. My husband informed me that everyone knew what coffer ceilings were. I didn't think so, so I did a scientific survey. I asked about a dozen of my friends and the majority of them did not know either.

If you also are not familiar with this type of ceiling, the ceiling slopes up gradually from the molding around the top of the wall. It then meets a rectangle of smaller molding. The rectangle in the center becomes the flat part of the ceiling. I look at the corner of the rectangle; a line seems to shoot down to meet the corner of the wall. Sometimes the lines and the corners don't seem to line up; then I put my glasses on or change my position a bit and everything is straight again. The fan turns in the center of the rectangle, interfering with shadows on the ceiling. I wonder how my ceiling would look with more decorative molding; possibly to pick up the mauve or teal in the wallpaper. Sometimes I lie and wonder how a mural would look on the flat rectangular part of the ceiling. I don't think I would be interested in a Michelangelo style. Maybe flowers would be nice. As I lie here I wonder what my room might look like with these changes.

I wonder how my life would be different if I had not gone into the Navy and what it would be like if I had stayed there. I wonder how my life would be different if I did not have multiple sclerosis.

BACK TO REALITY

I returned to Kingsburg where I lived with my parents. I did not get my old bedroom back since my younger sister who was now in high school had claimed it. I made my home in the back bedroom, secluded with my pain medications and chocolate milk shakes to gain weight.

I was still trying to figure out what was going on with my body, or was it my mind? Symptoms came and went and, at times, were very strange. One day my eyes might be affected, the next day I might feel numb. What a confusing ordeal. I was beginning to feel afraid.

THE V.A. EXPERIENCE

My father took me to my first visit to the Veterans Administration Hospital in Fresno, twenty miles north of our home in Kingsburg. At the time I was experiencing pain and weakness in my legs. Our first stop was the evaluation office. The woman at the desk kept telling me to stand up and my father to sit down. Since I was very good at following orders, I kept standing. My father kept saying, "No, sit down." So I was up and down and I was the one having problems with my legs. It dawned on us that she assumed that he was the patient. I certainly didn't look like the typical veteran. I still don't for that matter. This woman was used to seeing men a tad bit older than I going through her office. We assured her I was the patient. Only then would she permit me to take the seat in her office and let my father stand.

The doctors at the Fresno VA were greatly stumped with my case and they referred me to Fort Miley VA Hospital in San Francisco.

THE DIAGNOSIS

At Fort Miley, after many painful tests, I was diagnosed as having multiple sclerosis. MS is difficult to diagnose with modern diagnostic techniques. At that time it was even more difficult to diagnose. The definitive test for me was the painful spinal tap. MS does not always show up in this test; it always did for me.

The spinal tap is an experience in itself. This involves essentially what it sounds like. A huge needle is inserted in the spine and spinal fluid is removed for testing. After the test, it was recommended to me that I not raise my head for twenty-four hours to avoid headaches. After the recommended twenty-four hours, when I raised my head it felt as if it were being bounced off a cement floor. The severe headaches persisted for several days. The test showed elevated gamma globulin levels that apparently confirmed MS.

I was very pleased to have a diagnosis. Of course, I had no idea what MS was, but I assumed they would give me a pill or shot or something and I would be fine. After all, my Dad was a doctor. He made people well that way, right? I soon found out that I was wrong. There was and still is no cure for MS. They still don't even know what causes it. But I still had hope because these doctors could always be wrong.

SECOND OPINION

Since my family is originally from the Midwest, my father has a lot of faith in the Mayo Clinic in Rochester, Minnesota. Four years after my initial diagnosis, with my MS persistently progressing, he took me there for a second opinion. Unfortunately, after extensive, painful testing, which included the spinal tap, they came up with the same diagnosis. Apparently I did have MS.

WHEELIN' AND DEALIN'

The wheelchair is not necessarily a negative thing for me. Besides reducing falls, it has opened a lot of doors. There were places I did not go because it involved too much walking. The wheelchair reduced my fatigue level so I could do many more things. Now I could go shopping or even to the county fair.

While wheelchairs can obviously be beneficial, there are negative aspects about being in a wheelchair. The biggest negative is stairs. Where they exist without an accompanying ramp, I remain an outsider. Traveling may also be difficult in a wheelchair. Many people in wheelchairs can drive especially with the help of hand-controlled equipment. Some wheelchairs will fit in the back seat of the car, but since I use an electric wheelchair, I don't have that luxury. I had to trade in my new car (well, at least it was new for me) for a van with a wheelchair lift.

Traveling by air can be a traumatic experience. There are many transfers from one chair to another. A regular wheelchair will not fit down the aisle so I have to be transferred into an aisle chair which is very narrow. The aisle chair comes in several models. Personally, I prefer the older ones because they have a high back and can be tilted back so I do not feel as if I am falling forward. Once seated in this chair, I am strapped in securely and the person takes me to my seat. I am really not sure who is in charge of doing this, the airline or the airport. It seems to change or at least it has in the past. Even though airline travel in a wheelchair can be a trying experience, it is possible and the benefits are usually well worth it.

DEALIN' OR NOT DEALIN'

Everyone reacts to their MS, or any other disability for that matter, in a different way. We all have different coping mechanisms to deal with life's trials and tribulations. Dealing with a disability, including MS, is no exception. Just as MS symptoms differ from person to person the way people react to their MS also differs.

Although we do not have control over the course of our MS, we do have control over how we deal with it. I had this friend who was ambulatory. He had a limp and a foot drop that is common with MS. The muscles in the ankle do not support the foot so the toes drop downward often causing stumbling or even falling. This man was concerned that people would think he was drunk. He still refused to use a cane. One day we were talking. I was sitting in my wheelchair. He said, "If I ever had to be in a wheelchair, I'd kill myself." I automatically slapped my forehead and said, "Wow, my life ended and no one told me." Eventually this man had to turn to the use of a wheelchair for his mobility. The last I heard, he is still alive but very bitter and angry.

I recently saw a television show that told about a woman with MS who had committed suicide. Her husband said that her eyesight was failing. Her sense of taste had diminished and she could not walk. In fact, he added, she could not even crawl. This was a young woman and some would even say her symptoms were not that severe. This definitely shows the difference in how people react to this disease. I know lots of people who have MS who are very well-adjusted. In fact, they carry on normal, productive lives. These people are like anyone else, sometimes down and sad, and at other times up and happy.

ULTIMATE DEALIN'

I have been asked how I deal with my disease. As I look back, I am sure the Lord must have given me the gift to accept this crazy illness. Sometimes I cannot believe how quickly I adapt to the changes MS constantly brings into my life. I never gave myself the option of giving up. I certainly never considered suicide. I know some people with MS give up right after their diagnosis. I don't know why but even at different stages of my disability and even as it continues to progress, I never think of giving up.

When I finally worked through my anger with God, and was walking in His path, coping became easier. I don't mean to imply that it was easy. It just became easier. During painful times when I don't think I can handle it, I remember two things that make my situation more bearable. One is that God does not give us more than we can handle. 1 Corinthians 10:13 states:

> *"There hath no temptation taken you but such as is common to man: but God is faithful, who will not suffer you to be tempted above that ye are able; but will with the temptation also make a way to escape, that ye may be able to bear it."*
> *(King James version)*

In other words, I can be sure that I am not experiencing any temptation, trouble or painful circumstance that has not been experienced by others.

God is faithful. If He allows something to come into my life then I can be assured that it is bearable with His strength and His help. God knows our load limit and He will not permit us to carry more than our capacity.

Secondly, I think about how Jesus suffered because He loves me. I certainly did not and still do not deserve the grace of this wonderful gift. It is amazing to think that Jesus would have given His life even if I were the only one involved. What I experience is nothing compared to the suffering He went through on the cross for my eternal life.

CHAPTER EIGHT

DISCOVERING GOD AGAIN

As I lie in bed and look around my room, my eyes are drawn to my television set. It is something you can not miss because it has a forty-five inch screen.

I go through stages where at times I will watch a lot of TV and then I may not watch it for awhile. I used to watch for educational purposes but now I watch mainly for entertainment. As I look up at the fan, watching it move, I think about the times I was on TV. That was during what you might call my heyday of the 1980's. It was a time when I was very active. I was on several local TV talk shows and news programs talking about MS and various topics relating to my work. I enjoyed this part of my life. It was certainly not what I had anticipated. The Lord had a path for me and I was simply following along.

BACK TO SCHOOL

When I was discharged from the Navy I was at a loss as to what to do. A junior college was only about ten miles from my parents' home where I was living so I decided to take some classes there. At times this was not as easy as it sounds. The first semester my parents took turns driving me to school and then pushing me to my classes in a wheelchair. Mom would sit through classes with me. Although she really enjoyed it, I just couldn't get her to register as a student. She said, "That would make it work instead of fun." With a remission, which allowed me to walk again, school got easier. I graduated with my Associates degree in three years.

From there I went to California State University, Fresno and studied psychology. This was the most difficult part of my schooling since I was juggling school and my first marriage which was shaky. After about eight years, with my health going up and down, I finally graduated with a masters degree in clinical psychology.

MORE THAN AN INTERNSHIP

I then worked on an internship for about two years for my Marriage, Family and Child Counseling license. Part of this was at the Fresno County Juvenile Hall as a family therapist. I developed this new position but there was no individual office space available. I was placed in the Chaplain's office since he was often on business elsewhere. This provided me with a private place to see my clients. I was not sure how this was going to work out because, at the time, I was not walking with the Lord.

I imagined my office mate would be a very straight laced business-like preacher who would be doing exactly that, preaching at me. I figured he would not approve of my smoking and possibly some of my counseling techniques. My sessions did tend to get kind of loud at times. It is funny how some preconceived notions can be completely wrong.

I was shocked the first time I met Chaplain Ron. He did not look at all like I thought a chaplain would look. He wore blue jeans and a western belt with cowboy boots. His muscular arms supported several tattoos.

Ron and I did not see each other often, but when we did we would sit and talk. He did not preach at me, we just talked about a variety of topics. It was easy to talk with him. I am sure his social work background helped him to be a good listener.

During this time I was having a lot of trouble with pain and weakness in my legs. I had reached the point that my anger was directed at my body. I hated my legs. Ron helped me with all the resentment I had towards God and myself.

I don't remember exactly what Ron told me when I was complaining about my legs. I am sure it was more eloquent than the interpretation that I remember now. I remember him saying something along the lines that you are fortunate to have your legs. You can stand on them to transfer from one chair to another. If nothing else, they serve an aesthetic value. Your clothing fits much better now than if you had no legs. I must admit that Ron made sense. When I started to look at the more positive value of my legs, they seemed to hurt less. I know my anger at my body decreased.

YOU CAN NOT RUN AWAY

I don't remember Ron and I speaking directly about my anger at God, but through our talks that anger subsided. For years I was like Jonah who tried to run away from God; then Jonah concluded that there was no way to do so. God was still always with him. God, too, was always with me. Even though I left Him at times, He never left me. This concept is exemplified in the following beautiful poem:

"Footprints"

*One night I had a dream. I was
walking along a beach with the Lord,
and across the sky flashed scenes
from my life. In each scene,
I noticed two sets of footprints,
side by side in the sand.*

*One was mine and one was the Lord's.
When the last scene of my life
appeared before me, I looked back,
and to my surprise, I saw that
during the lowest
and saddest times of my life, there
was only one set of footprints.
"Lord," I cried, "you said that once I
decided to follow you, you would walk
beside me all the way.
But during the most troublesome times
in my life there is only one set
of footprints. I don't understand
why you left my side
when I needed you the most."
The Lord turned and looked at me,
His eyes filled with love.
"My precious child," He said.
"I have never left you.
During your times of trial, where
you only see one set of footprints,
that was when I was carrying you."*

I understood the author of this poem was unknown. At first I thought, what a shame not to know who wrote this beautiful poem. Then I realized this author has surely been blessed by touching so many people with this beautiful work. Then one miracle after another occurred. It was brought to my attention that Guidepost (July 1992 magazine) reported that Hallmark cards had attributed the authorship of "Footprints" to Margaret R. Powers of Coquitlan, British Columbia, Canada. One of the things that convinced Hallmark cards that Margaret was the author was that she had written the poem in her wedding album the day she married Paul Powers. Thank you, Margaret R. Powers for sharing these lovely thoughts with us.

I realized God could handle all the anger I had directed towards Him in the past. In fact, He even forgave me for my misdirected anger. It was not God's fault. In Romans 8:28 Paul states,

"And we know that all that happens to us is working for our good if we love God and are fitting into his plans."
(Living Bible)

God had a plan for me and I was starting to accept that plan whatever it might be.

CHAPTER NINE

LOVE, HONOR AND CHERISH

As I lie in bed looking around my room, my eyes focus on the bed post at the foot of the bed. I have a four poster bed. The bed post stands rather high above the foot board. The carving is nice but not real intricate. At the top sits a ball. It was hard for me to find a king-sized cannonball bed so I had this one made in cherry wood. I had decided, and my husband agreed, that I would sleep near the center of the bed to avoid possibly rolling out. That sounded good in theory, but in practice I tend to scoot more to my original left side of the bed. Although I want to be near my husband, I guess I consider anything over the center line to be his space. Maybe my belief of having distinct sides of the bed is just my nature or possibly I learned it. It may relate to when I shared the bed with my sister as a child. We would draw an imaginary line down the center of the bed, never to be touched or crossed. The ultimate consequence was a parental scolding after one of us would yell "She's on my side!" Ultimately, it looks like I learned the "my side of the bed" rule from my parents.

I think we learn a lot about marriage from our parents. I always assumed my marriage would be like my parents' marriage. Actually, I thought most marriages were that way. I never knew my parents to fight or even argue as far as that goes. They may have had disagreements, but I never even saw those. I would later find that some marriages are not that way.

DIVORCE

Statistics report a fifty percent divorce rate. Some studies have shown as high as an 82% divorce rate in marriages where one partner has a chronic illness. MS being a chronic illness, would be included in these results. Not everyone agrees with these statistics.

The National Multiple Sclerosis Society contends there is no or minimal difference in the rate of divorce between MS marriages and the general population. I propose that the divorce rate in MS marriages is probably somewhere between the two figures of 50% and 82%. This higher rate is probably due to several factors. One, the healthy partner cannot accept the disease or what the disease might become. The second factor seems to be that the person with the disease drives their partner away, probably due to a low self-image.

My first marriage occurred in 1976 when I was able to cover my disease well and appear relatively healthy. It ended in divorce about two years later. Although he would blame my illness for our problems, I don't believe that for a minute. The real reason for our divorce, I believe, was that he could not remember where his bed was. I believe our divorce had nothing to do with the fact that I happened to have MS.

A SECOND CHANCE

God knew about me, my MS and what it would become. He knew I would need a strong partner by my side to help me through it. One of the biggest miracles of my life occured on March 2, 1982, when I met Eric Silvius. He was introduced to me by my sister Renee and her significant other (who later became her husband). I looked perfectly healthy at the time, but I saw no reason to keep my illness a secret. After one fun-filled date, Eric invited me out again at which time I told him about my MS. His response to me was, "So what? I have hay fever." This was not negating the seriousness of MS; rather he was saying it was not a determining factor in our relationship. At the time, he really knew very little about MS. Over the years Eric has become what I consider to be an expert on the subject.

THE PERFECT MARRIAGE

    Needless to say our relationship got serious, and then more serious, until the following February 26th we were married. The wedding ceremony characterizes our personalities. We had a surprise wedding in the middle of a birthday party for my nephews. Eric and I left the party for awhile and returned in our wedding attire. We were accompanied by a preacher, a best man and maid of honor. I was wearing my mother's wedding gown. This was not a spur of the moment wedding for Eric and me. We chose this time because my grandparents were visiting from Iowa, and Eric's parents were here from Kansas. Being the practical people we are, we decided this was a good time. Actually, Eric and I were, and are, more serious about this commitment than it may sound. This may be due to our being a little older and wiser in some ways.
    Although Eric had a religious background he was not a Christian. This was not an issue for me since I was not walking with the Lord at the time. When I went back to the Lord this became an issue about which I continue to pray.

ONE PLUS ONE EQUALS TOGETHER

The first year of our marriage was shaky for me health-wise. I seemed to be going downhill. All of the while Eric continued to support me even when I started using a wheelchair. This was shortly after our first anniversary. He had encouraged me to get an electric wheelchair a few months before so that we could go to the county fair. Eric has never considered the MS to be "my" problem. He has always considered it to be something that we dealt with together as a couple.

Eric and I both had our own careers and interests. We were never dependent on each other to fulfill our individual needs. Neither of us dominated the other. I did not need Eric to define who I was nor did he need me to define who he was.

I actively pursued my career as a family therapist. The wheelchair did not stop me; in fact, it actually helped me because it allowed me to sustain activity longer. Eric also continued to pursue his career in business. This enabled us to be closer as a couple since we both had interests to share.

SILENT STRUGGLES

After Eric and I were married for about six years, my MS progressed further. I continued my work but at a much slower pace. As usual, Eric was standing by me, working with the doctors. He was even able to come up with some great ideas, such as an idea to help support my arms to ease the pain of paralyzed shoulders.

When I lost my voice, Eric and I had to go through a lot of adjustments. First, I had to stop working in the job for which I had trained so long. It had never really seemed like work because I enjoyed it so much.

Secondly, I couldn't converse with Eric which put a real damper on our relationship. Joy was scarce for both of us as our struggles increased. It was as if we no longer had each other to share our problems with. Without realizing it I "crashed" into a deep state of depression. I withdrew, essentially "vegetated" and became a non-person. I was very frustrated. My attempts at whispering and mouthing words were either incomprehensible or misinterpreted. These were very strenuous and ineffective ways of communicating.

Eric and his secretary developed a rudimentary letter board for me. This was dependent on people's ability to spell as well as my ability to move my arms and hands. Although this was a slow process, it was all we had going for us at the time. Out of necessity Eric and I developed some sign language but it was pretty much our own. Not many others could understand what I was trying to say.

COMMUNICATION RETURNS

About six months after I lost my voice I was introduced to an electric voice apparatus. Although I could not operate it myself, it had a dramatic effect on my life. After the first day I used this, Eric remarked, "It's like you got your personality back."

All of a sudden I realized what condition I had really been in for the last few months. I had been in a state of severe depression, shock and denial. Even though this instrument was not perfect, it was a vehicle for conversation and communication, especially with my husband. As the depression lessened, Eric and I were able to work through some issues that had been put off for too long.

HUMOR

We really had to rely on our sense of humor at this point. Eric had his career, but I did not. I found myself living through him for a while, and neither of us wanted that. I did have my faith in God. This had always pulled me through before. I held on tight and said, "Lord, don't leave me now." With His help I was able to get a life again.

When I was more able-bodied I was determined not to turn my husband into my caregiver. He was to be my partner, my lover. Now that we are faced more with caregiving issues, I see what a struggle this can be. We are grateful to have some good helpers, but there are always emergency situations where Eric must take on this role for a short time. Fortunately, he is a person that can easily switch back when the emergency is over.

One thing that keeps us going is a sense of humor. It is important in all situations but especially when there is a disability. It is powerful in turning around what appears to be an inescapable problem. Humor may be a key factor in keeping any marriage healthy. It works for us. It has been an essential factor in keeping Eric and me on solid ground through some shaky times.

I am convinced that God in his miraculous way sent Eric to me. He knew I would need this strong man by my side as my illness progressed.

CHAPTER TEN

THE ROUTE TO CHURCH

As I lie in bed my eyes are drawn to a small octagonal plaque that hangs on the wall to the left of me. Pink is the color of the padded water-marked taffeta frame. There are also pink cloth rose buds and a ribbon on the upper left of the frame, surrounded by a small taffeta ruffle. In the center is the following verse:

> *"He shall give His angels charge over thee,*
> *to keep thee in all thy ways."*
>
> Psalm 91:11

My friend Patti gave this plaque to me. I met Patti through teaching her daughter in Sunday School.

INTRODUCTION

It's funny how sometimes you meet a person and they introduce you to someone else who introduces you to someone else. Actually, it could be a person, place or thing to which they introduce you. Not only was that the way I met Patti, Leslie set off this same chain reaction for me. She was a probation officer at Juvenile Hall and a strong Christian woman. Through her, I met David, who is the founder of Valley Teen Ranch. Valley Teen Ranch is a Christian group home for troubled boys. At the time I met him, they were in the planning stages of the ranch. David and his wife had gone through extensive training and had worked at the original Teen

Ranch in Michigan. I began working with David on the psychological component for the ranch.

There was a big demand for parenting assistance and David got a lot of calls asking for his help. We saw a tremendous need. Since it would be awhile before the ranch would be ready to open, we began to do a few Christian parenting talks. Most of our presentations were done at churches.

I was introduced to St. Luke's United Methodist Church when we gave a talk there. The church looked wheelchair accessible and I even saw people there I knew. I thought I might be interested in attending. There was something missing from my life. I thought I knew what it was but I was not yet willing to admit that it was an active Christian life.

TOUCHSTONES

I had several touchstones for returning to church. A touchstone is what appeals to us about something which leads us to a specific action. In my work as a therapist, I sometimes helped clients establish their goals. One exercise I used was to ask them, "If you had five lives to live how would you live each life?" Then I assure them that, "No, I have no inside information. You do not have five lives so you must put the touchstone of each life into one life." I asked them, "What appeals to you about that life?" That is the touchstone.

I did this exercise with my sister. In one of her lives, she wanted to be a cowgirl. When I asked her what appealed to her about being a cowgirl, she quickly responded, "I like cowboys." That was the touchstone for her.

The touchstones for me for going back to church, at least the ones I had identified, were the fellowship and music. The specific church that I went to had what was called

Midweek Miracle. This consisted of dinner and a Bible study. The dinner was the touchstone for me because I found the idea of going to church and eating very appealing. When I went to Midweek Miracle I also joined a Bible study group that was already in progress. They were studying Ephesians when I joined them. Ephesians 4:11 really started my thinking. It states,

> *"It was he who gave some to be apostles, some to be prophets, some to be evangelists and some to be pastors and teachers."*
>
> *(NIV)*

I later read more about gifts in Romans 12:6-8. In this passage Paul relays:

> *"We have different gifts, according to the grace given us. If a man's gift is prophesying, let him use it in proportion to his faith. If it is serving, let him serve; if it is teaching, let him teach; if it is encouraging, let him encourage; if it is contributing to the needs of others, let him generously; if it is leadership, let him govern diligently; if it is showing mercy, let him do it cheerfully."*
>
> *(NIV)*

Wow! If God gives special gifts I wonder if He even gave one to me. That was something that was heavy on my mind for a while. I thought about it and I prayed about it, until the answer finally came to me. My profession was counseling which always came naturally to me. I saw counseling as my spiritual gift from God. I felt that I was doing what God wanted me to do.

NOW WHAT?

Then one Saturday night I got a phone call. It was a client who was in the process of committing suicide. I called the emergency people who got him to the hospital. He lived. The next morning I went to church. During the altar call at the final hymn, I went to the altar and prayed, "Lord, what do I do next? You gave me this gift but what is going on?"

The response I seemed to have received was that I could not do anymore with this man. It was not up to me to do it all, God had to intervene. I was getting a bit cocky with this gift and had neglected to include God where I needed Him.

Now I use the 33.3% rule in my therapy - my clients do 33.3% of the work; I do 33.3% of the work and God does 33.3% of the work. The remaining 0.1% is negotiable. We can only do it with God in my sessions. It is not uncommon for me to pray with some of my clients if I deem it to be appropriate and it is what the client needs or requests at the time. During times of silence I may simply take a deep breath and say a silent prayer asking for God's presence and guidance. When things get real heavy, I might go to my desk which leaves me in a position where my back is turned toward the couch where my client or clients are sitting. Since at that point my clients are unaware of what important business I might be engaged in, I have some time with the Lord to seek which direction our session should go next.

In Tony Campolo's tape, (1982), he refers to the Hans-Eisnich study. According to this study, patients in the first year of psychoanalysis will show a 44% improvement. With psychotherapy, patients improve at a rate of 53% in the first year. Patients receiving psychiatric help improve 61% during the first year. Surprising to many psychotherapists, patients not receiving any form of treatment show a 73% improvement. I have a theory about this. No, I have no study to back my ideas. This is just something to which I have given some thought. I wonder if the rate of the improvement has something to do with the presence of God in these sessions and the lives of these people? Just a thought.

Now back to my suicidal client. I did not desert him when he went into the hospital. In fact, his psychiatrist called me and requested that I come to the hospital to work with this man. Apparently, my former client had made it clear he would not talk to anyone but me about his problems. I visited him several times.

Frank had been the worship leader that traumatic Sunday I went to the altar. He had prayed with me for the healing of this man. On one occasion Frank accompanied me to the hospital. At my request, he had made an audio tape of a solo that had been sung during the worship service. I thought this might be relevant to and help my client. We took the tape and tape player with us on our visit. The song title was "Give Them All to Jesus" by Phil Johnson. The part of the song that I was most touched by was:

"Give them all to Jesus -shattered dreams,
wounded hearts and broken toys;
Give them all, give them all,
give them all to Jesus;
And He will turn your sorrow into joy."

I do not know if the patient we were visiting was touched by this song as much as Frank and I were, nor do I know if this man is a Christian today. All I can do is to pray for him.

My reconnection with God and the church certainly helped me with my counseling. It also tied up a lot of loose ends in my life.

Paul reminds us in Hebrews 10:25:

"Let us not give up meeting together, as some are in the habit of doing, but let us encourage one another—and all the more as you see the Day approaching."

Not only is joining together an opportunity to encourage each other but it also holds us accountable to one another.

CHAPTER ELEVEN

THE LORD IS MY SHEPHERD

As I lie in bed and look around my room my eyes are drawn to a silver frame on the wall. It contains calligraphy style writing of the 23rd Psalm. It is done in purple ink with pink and purple flowers in the corner, surrounded by green leaves. In each place where the words "my" or "I" are found in this Biblical Psalm, my name has been substituted. In other words my verse reads: "The Lord is Penny's shepherd; Penny shall not want..." I have found this to be very beneficial for me in my life. I would definitely recommend that you sit down and rewrite the 23rd Psalm substituting your name. This really makes it more personal and assures us that we are not alone.

The section "Yea, though Penny walks through the valley of the shadow of death, Penny will fear no evil for thou art with Penny;" has been comforting to me during bad times. As I read that or someone reads it to me, peace flows through me.

I certainly could have used this version of the 23rd Psalm to impress upon my heart years before I received the gift of this lovely calligraphy work. It might have been a little easier to deal with some comments relating to my disease. I understand that many people who made these remarks meant well and were just trying to help but they still hurt at times.

GIMP SINNER

One day my husband, my parents and I were at a restaurant. As I recall, it was not a fancy place. Everyone was sitting in a booth and I was pulled up to the end in my wheelchair. A man that I didn't know came up to me and said,

"If you would only pray for healing, God would heal you and you would not be in this wheelchair." I gave him a small smile and turned back to the people with whom I was dining. He said something else which I didn't get, probably because I was feeling uncomfortable about our interruption. I got the feeling my family was uncomfortable also. I felt conspicuous, as if I had a neon sign on my back which said, "Gimp sinner." (Gimp is a derogatory term for a physically disabled person.)

What a new concept this man had. He suggested that I pray for healing as if I had not heard that before. Okay, maybe this man was only trying to help but I was perturbed. Was I perturbed at this man, God, or both? I really don't know. All I know is that, as a devoted Christian, I had spent many hours praying for healing.

GOD HEALS...IN HIS WAY

I was upset. Was there a reason God was not healing me? Was I doing something wrong? Didn't God hear my prayers? Wasn't He listening? I knew God could heal, why wasn't He healing me? What was so terrible about me? I was, again, questioning myself, God and my relationship with Him.

The next day I got on the phone and called Pastor Al. (Pastor Al refers to Dr. Alvern Vom Steeg, who was then the Pastor of St. Luke's United Methodist Church in Fresno, CA.) "Emergency, emergency, come right away." He came over, and I explained to him the emergency.

Pastor Al shed light upon the different ways the Lord heals. There are definitely miracle healings as are described throughout the New Testament. Now, that's what I wanted - a miracle healing! It's proven all through the New Testament that the Lord can do it, so I was still asking, "Why not me, Lord?"

There are times the Lord heals slowly as is described with the blind man in Mark 8:22-25. When Jesus touched the blind man's eyes he could see, but not clearly. The second time Jesus touched his eyes he saw clearly. Now, I could even handle that! I just wanted some progress, some sign that my healing was starting.

With the Lord's help, healing also occurs through doctors and other health professionals. I did not find this real encouraging. It had become quite clear to me this was not happening in my case. The doctors were at a loss. They had no idea what to do.

Pastor Al emphasized that God begins healing at the point of our greatest need. That's it! That's what I had been looking for and that's what had been happening with me. Christ had begun to heal me at the point of my greatest need. Although I still had multiple sclerosis and I was still in a wheelchair, I had received healing from God. I still have a lot of pain and limitations. In fact, someone who didn't know me well would not notice the healing that has occurred over time.

God had healed me at the point of my greatest need, which was to have peace and acceptance with my illness. My situation is certainly different with Christ in my life. I feel much more at peace. I know I am not alone and that there is a purpose for my physical condition. I can't begin to compare what I feel to the tremendous suffering that Jesus experienced when He died for my sins on the cross. I now feel more of an empathy with Him and a closeness to Him because of the pain in my own life. Even as my illness progresses, I continue to feel peace because I know He holds my future in His hands.

I used to pray to be healed.
But now I pray that
God will use me.
Today, I feel that God

has healed me from
The need to be healed.
Charlie Wedemeyer

GOD HEALS...IN HIS TIME

I definitely believe that God heals. I also believe this healing will take place in His time and in His way. There is a conflicting belief by some Christians I have heard called the Name it and Claim it Philosophy. They believe if you pray for something, God will give you exactly what you ask for when you ask for it. In other words, if you pray for complete healing, God will give exactly that - a complete healing. It just does not work that way. Can you imagine how chaotic the world would be if everyone got what they prayed for exactly how they prayed for it and when they prayed for it? We need to have faith in our Lord to know what is best for us. We need to recognize that the answer to our prayers may indeed be "yes." But the answer may also be "no" or "wait." God has a good reason for it. Even though we probably do not understand the reason, we still need to accept it to be the best answer.

THE ULTIMATE HEALING

As mentioned earlier, Pastor Al introduced the concept to me that another form of healing which God performs is through death. I later became more enlightened about this concept from Michel Bucci. He was a man in our congregation who was attending graduate school under a Canadian visa. Michel was a high level quadriplegic whose neck was broken in a trampoline accident. He had no movement below his neck and had used a wheelchair for many years. I heard Michel speak once at church, referring to his condition as being temporary. He explained that when he left this earth to go home with the Lord he would not be in a wheelchair. He would have a new body. This was a revelation to me. If Michel was going to get a new body in heaven, then maybe I would too. (Note: Michel received his new body on March 25th, 1993.)

I searched in my Bible and it said in II Corinthians 5, that I would be getting a wonderful new body in heaven. My spirit will not just be floating around, it will be in a heavenly body—with no pain. I am going to be healthy. I am sure I will be dancing down the golden streets of heaven. I will probably even be doing Jazzercise.

I also understand, from the book of Revelation, that I will be singing in a choir of millions. Not with the voice I have now, but with a beautiful voice. In one of David Jeremiah's sermons entitled, "What Heaven Will Be Like," he talks about serving God. Although we serve God here on earth, we fall short of perfection. In heaven we will be serving Him perfectly. We will be joyfully serving the Lord in a capacity that we enjoy. We will never tire of it. I think of what I would enjoy doing to serve God. I enjoy counseling but I can not imagine there being a need for counselors in a perfect place like heaven. I'll just have to wait to see what service the Lord has in mind for me.

The way I see it, heaven is going to be a busy place, at least for me. I'll enjoy it that way. I will be doing my dancing and singing and whatever service the Lord sees fit for me to do. I am also looking forward to a tremendous feast. We will all be reunited with old friends who have gone home before us. What a joy it will be to see family members and even those whom I have just heard about because they lived generations before me. I am sure there will also be times for rest of some sort in heaven. Even God rested on the seventh day.

As I was explaining my idea of heaven to a friend, he rather sarcastically said, "Wow, it sounds like you've been there!" I responded that of course I had not, but with what I have read and with God's promise that all will be fulfilled, this is what I imagined. I certainly don't have all the details right since heaven is too wonderful for us to imagine. It's impossible for us to explain the unexplainable —and heaven is certainly the unexplainable. Even after seeing his clear vision of heaven, the Apostle John was unsuccessful in attempting to describe it. When you see me there, feel free to point out how I imagined it differently. Then we can both laugh about how much more glorious heaven is than we had even imagined.

GOD'S WORK IS REVEALED

One day while working at Juvenile Hall, I was talking with a unit counselor with whom I had minimal contact. We met only to discuss a few mutual cases. I had been in a wheelchair for about a year but he chose this time to relay his thoughts about my condition. He explained to me his belief that it was not the work of the Lord that I was in a wheelchair but that I had the devil in me. I returned to my office in tears for a couple of reasons. First, I was shocked that some people might be perceiving me this way. Secondly, I had an unreasonable fear that this man might be right. I talked with my friend, Leslie, who worked there as a probation officer. She calmed me down enough so that I could drive home. She also canceled the rest of my appointments for the day.

Again, I got on the phone and called Pastor Al. "Emergency, emergency, come right away." Pastor Al arrived and listened to my crisis. He gave me a verse that better helped me to understand my problem. The verse was John 9:1-3. Jesus sure smashed the concept that illness and disease are caused by an individual's sin when He responded to the question of why a man was blind. His response was that it was not that anyone has sinned "But to demonstrate the power of God." That convinced me that the devil is not in me and that my illness is not the work of the devil. I believe it was at that point that I became aware that there was a reason for my disability. I am not at all convinced that God gave me this disability, but I believe He will use it for good. Like Jesus had said with the blind man, I believed my disability would be used to demonstrate the power of God How? I wasn't sure, but I was beginning to have more faith in the Lord.

As I look back on my "emergency" calls, I wonder how and why Pastor Al dropped everything to come when I called. He had a large congregation and I was not even a member of the church at that time. As I think back, I realize how important his visits were to my Christian growth. I might have drifted away from God again if Pastor Al had not been there to be my spiritual guide. He obviously knew this. I am sure his direct line to God made him aware of how fragile I was during these times.

THE LORD IS GLORIFIED

"My grace is sufficient for thee; for my strength is made perfect in weakness."
(II Corinthians 12:9, King James Version)

I am here to demonstrate the power of the Lord. I have a cross to bear, but the Lord is helping me. I am experiencing the Lord in different ways through my disability, ways that I do not think would be possible otherwise. I am thankful for things which I may not have even noticed before. I find myself pausing throughout the day to have a chat with the Lord. This may be a time of thanks, asking for strength or a time of questioning which way to turn. I find my relationship with my savior becoming stronger each day. I know I need His strength more when I am at my weakest. This is when I feel the Lord's presence the most.

MEMBERSHIP AND MORE

On Sunday, October 19, 1986, I joined St. Luke's United Methodist Church in Fresno, California. This occurred after a nine week class consisting of nine sessions where we learned about the church and what membership really means. My membership Sunday was certainly important for me. My husband sat at my right side while my parents were at my left. This was exciting and different from attending church by myself as was my normal routine.

There were about a dozen people from my class joining the church that day. Pastor Al placed his hand on each of our heads and prayed for us individually. He sure must have studied us during our classes since he knew exactly the right words to say for each person. After the pastor welcomed us into the church we turned and faced the congregation who also welcomed us. We then took our seats and church service proceeded as normal but things were not as they normally were. I was different; I was beaming; something monumental had just occurred. I wanted to say out loud:

"Excuse me. Excuse me, Pastor Al, I'm not sure everyone is aware of what just happened here. There were more than just a few prayers and congratulations. I have been coming to this church for several years. I had asked Jesus into my life and into my heart many years ago, but today was different. I gave my life to Jesus today. I am not the same person. I certainly do not feel the same. I just thought you should know. Go ahead with what you have planned. Thank you for listening."

    I obviously did not say this. I calmed down a little bit where I was not so bubbly but, fortunately, the feeling never left me totally. I still have my ups and downs, but since that day, the ups seem to be more up and the downs don't seem to be quite as far down. I feel Jesus is with me and nothing can come between us anymore.

"For I am persuaded, that neither death, nor life, nor angels, nor principalities, nor powers, nor things present, nor things to come, nor height, nor depth, nor any other creature, shall be able to separate us from the love of God, which is in Christ Jesus our Lord."
(Romans 8:38-39 KJV)

CHAPTER TWELVE

MY CONFUSION, NOT GOD'S

As I lie in bed looking around my room I notice how cluttered it might seem to other people. I like to have things around me at which to look. Many of these things I consider to be pretty, some trigger memories, others are just junk that needs to be put away.

Today, my dresser may look more cluttered than usual since it has three bouquets of flowers added. There is not a special occasion for these flowers. Well, I guess one of them is for a special occasion. It is a Halloween arrangement of fall colors. I have never had flowers of this kind. They are brown, yellow, gold, auburn and other fall colors. The container is a brown rectangular dish with the words "Trick" and "Treat" on the long sides and the word "or" on the short sides. I had this arrangement for three days before I realized it had two small wooden witches stuck in it.

In the center of my dresser, the arrangement is in a large oval basket. The flowers of this arrangement are brighter with the main colors being yellow, purple, pink and fuschia.

The end bouquet is of white mini-mums. Judy brings them to me often. She picks them from either her yard or her mother's yard.

You may ask, "Why do these people bring me flowers all of the time?" I really do not have a good answer for this. They must like me but, sometimes I also ask myself why? "Why do they like me so much that they bring me flowers or other gifts?" I take delight in the attention and certainly want people to like me but I still ask, "Why?" This is just one of the little whys I ask.

WHY?

Have you ever asked God, "Why?" Yes? I didn't think I was the only one. I used to ask God Why? a lot. That used to go through my head, "Why me, Lord? Why do I have this disease? Why do I have this pain? Why did this happen to me? Why?" I knew God had the power to cure me. God had the desire, so what was He waiting for? Even when I was praying my Why? prayers, I was learning to listen. I just did not seem to be getting answers to my Why? questions.

A LOOK BACK

God may actually have been answering my Why prayers sooner than I thought. The problem was that the answer was not what I expected nor was it what I wanted. Therefore, I had not heard His answer until He put it in such an abrupt way that I could not possibly ignore it.

Now, I do not remember through what medium the answer to my Why prayers finally came. It might have been on television, the radio or even a sermon on tape. The preacher clearly stated the answer to my prayers. When I heard it, I knew this was the answer for which I had been listening. The answer was "IT'S NONE OF YOUR BUSINESS." That's right, it's none of my business.

God has his plan for the world and for me. He does not have to clear it with me first. Jeremiah 29:11 (Living Bible) tells us,

> "For I know the plans I have for you, says the Lord. They are plans for good and not for evil, to give you a future and a hope."

Let us suppose He did explain His plan to me. I would not understand anyway. Isaiah 55:9 says:

> *"For as the heavens are higher than the earth, so are my ways higher than your ways, and my thoughts than your thoughts."*

It's reassuring for me to know that God's thoughts are higher than mine since He's the One running the universe.

There are many aspects about God that I do not understand. Case in point—there is no time factor related to God. There is no past, present or future. Although He has given us free choice, He knows what that choice is going to be before we even make it because He knows the future. Now, this concept is very confusing to me. Does it baffle anyone else, or is it just me? God has the big plan for the entire world. Deuteronomy 29:29 states:

> *"The secret things belong unto the Lord our God; but those things which are revealed belong unto us and to our children forever, that we may do all the words of this law."*
>
> *(King James Version)*

So it looks like we need to be concerned about the things that have been revealed to us in the Holy Bible and to follow His words. That's certainly enough for us to deal with. We can be content letting the secret things belong unto the Lord our God.

Now, don't get me wrong. I have certainly not perfected this concept of not asking why? At times, I will still ask God why Jesus even asked God why when He was on the cross. He asked,

MIRACLES IN THE DARNDEST WAYS

"My God, my God, why has Thou forsaken Me?"
(Matthew 27:46b, Mark 15:34b, King James Version)

I guess that it is part of the human condition, to wonder why. Jesus was experiencing his humanness at that time. I am still working on reducing my why questions to God. I just need to keep reminding myself that He knows better than I do and that He does not have to clear His plans with me first.

JESUS IS GOD

Another concept with which I had extreme problems was how can Jesus be God. I did not know that this was a Biblical fact when I first heard it in church. I was so disturbed by this that I even stopped attending church until I got this figured out in my head. My sister's father-in-law, who is a Presbyterian minister, was visiting from Virginia. I sat down and discussed my confusion with him. He told me a story that helped me a lot. If you have this same confusion, maybe it will also help you.

There were three boys, on a summer day, intrigued by watching ants carrying food from one side of a rock to the other side. One boy remarked, "I wish I could tell them about this crack in the middle of the rock so they would not have to carry the food so far."

The other boy responded, "You would have to become an ant in order to do that."

This is the same concept that God used in sending His Son, Jesus, to earth in order that we would not be ignorant about what God can do for us. Through Jesus, He showed us the straight path to God. I am not saying that now I understand everything about this miraculous concept of the Trinity. I am saying that I understand it a little better and some of my confusion has decreased.

GOD IS EVERYWHERE

God is omnipresent. He is at all places at all times. This is an idea that is difficult, if not impossible for most or even all humans to understand. It is an idea that is not present in our human situations or experiences. In my church we have a time for silent prayer which is
followed by the pastoral prayer. I used to try to be finished with my silent prayer when the pastor began praying. I did not want to confuse God by having both of us praying at the same time. This was surely a self-centered thought. I considered myself to be one and everyone else, collectively, to be one. As I thought about this more, I realized that there were over a hundred people in my church alone saying their own silent prayers at the same time. There are over a hundred Christian churches in Fresno and I am sure many of them were in the process of praying at the same time we were. Then consider the entire country. How many people must have been praying to God at the same time? In other countries around the world, I am sure they were praying too. Millions of people are praying at the same time and God hears them all. He hears them all equally. He does not screen one out and say, "Well, Penny's prayer is more important than Patti's, so I will listen to Penny and not Patti." That is just not how God and His omnipresence works. He sees us all as equally important and our needs as equally important also. Fortunately, He has time for all of us. In fact, He has more time for us than we give to Him.

MIRACLES IN THE DARNDEST WAYS

LISTEN—YOU MAY BE SURPRISED AT WHAT YOU HEAR

Another thing I have found is it is very important to listen. I talk to God a lot, I am sure He is talking to me in His own way, if I will only listen. It is important that I communicate my needs to God. The Bible instructs us to do exactly this in Philippians 4:6. This passage reads,

"Do not be anxious about anything, but in everything by prayer and petition, with thanksgiving, present your requests to God."

(NIV)

After communicating our needs to God, the next logical step is to sit back and but listen to what His answers are.

I believe very much that God answers prayer. Sometimes His answer is "Yes." At other times the answer may be "No" or "Not now, but later." I certainly do not know His reasoning but His answers are not always what I want them to be. This reminds me of another story. I am not sure where I first heard this so I do not know to whom to give the credit.

This man was in a flood. I believe it was in the Midwest, but I'm not sure. It really does not make a lot of difference to the story anyway. The flood waters were rising and people were evacuating the area. Some friends of his in a raft went by and said "Get on board."

His reply was, "No, the Lord will save me." The waters continued to rise and the man began to climb the trellis on the side of his house.

Some people came by in a motor boat and yelled "Get on board."

Again, his reply was "No, the Lord will save me." The waters continued to rise and the man was forced to the top of his house.

A helicopter came by and someone shouted "Grab onto this rope and we will take you to safety."

Again, the man's reply was "No, the Lord will save me." The flood waters continued to rise and the man drowned. He went to heaven and talked to the Lord. Now that is how I imagine heaven. I will go straight to God and confront Him about the things I think He did wrong. Anyway, this guy goes to God and says, "What happened? Why didn't You save me from the flood?"

God responded, "I sent a raft, a boat and a helicopter. What else did you want?"

Sometimes I think that is how we look at prayer. When our prayers are not answered precisely as our request is made, we assume God is not answering or even listening to our prayers. That's how it was for me. Since God had not provided me with total physical healing, I questioned whether He was listening to me. I was wrong. God is always listening to us and He is always answering our prayers.

CHAPTER THIRTEEN

REGRETS

As I lie in bed looking around my room I focus upon my tape player on the night stand to my left. I listen to a lot of books on tape. My clock radio used to be in the place my tape player is now occupying. As the radio woke me up each morning, the music would continue playing until I was ready to leave for work. I don't listen to much music now. As I lie back and turn my focus to the fan above I think of some of the songs that I used to listen to. I know most of the words and concentrate on a few that have meaning to my life now. There is this one song - I do not know who wrote it and I am not sure who sang it. Frank Sinatra may have been the artist. It sounds like something he might have sung. I do not even remember song titles, but it goes something like this:

Regrets,
I've had a few,
but then again,
too few to mention.

Yes, I'm sure we all have had our share of regrets and most of us probably have had more than just a few.

SMALL REGRETS

There are regrets that need not be mentioned. I mean little things like: "I wish I had gone to my senior prom," or "I wish I had traveled more when I was able." These are regrets that affect no one but ourselves. They are over and done with and cannot be changed. Maybe some of the small regrets do involve others. For instance, I regret not having spent more time with my grandfather while he was alive. Although this did involve him at the time, it obviously does not affect him now that he is with the Lord. Again, it becomes my personal regret to deal with.

As I think about these regrets more, there may be a purpose in mentioning them. In sharing them with others, possibly people who are younger, it might prevent them from having the same regrets. But, then again, has there ever been a time when someone told you something in an attempt to spare you pain? Then, by not heeding their warning, you went through the avoidable discomfort. I know this has happened with me. Sometimes, maybe due to stubbornness or the attitude that "that was you but it will be different with me," we just have to learn on our own. Hopefully, one of the things we learn is to listen to others and learn from their experiences.

There may be other small regrets that involve others and may continue to affect them. For example, have you ever said an unkind word to someone that you later regretted? I know this has happened to me before. Then there is a dilemma. Do you bring the matter up and apologize or will this act just make matters worse? Each situation needs to be evaluated separately, of course, with consideration for the other person and a lot of prayer to guide you.

BIG REGRETS

Then there are those big regrets that may need to be disclosed; maybe not mentioned to another person, but at least communicated to God. Perhaps those are the regrets that involve sin. One of the Ten Commandments, as listed in Exodus 20, may have been broken. These sacred commandments are:

1. *I am the Lord your God. You shall have no other Gods before me.*
2. *You shall not worship any graven image.*
3. *You shall not take the name of the Lord your God in vain.*
4. *Remember to keep holy the Sabbath day.*
5. *Honor your father and mother.*
6. *You shall not kill.*
7. *You shall not commit adultery.*
8. *You shall not steal.*
9. *You shall not bear false witness against your neighbor.*
10. *You shall not covet anything that is your neighbor's.*
(From Children's Stories of the Bible.)

Are these the only sins? I think not. There may be felt sins. Anything you feel is coming between you and your relationship with God may be a sin. I do not think this is the same for everyone. It may even be something good like sports, hobbies or clubs. If it takes up so much of your time and thought that it pushes the Lord from your life, this may be a felt sin for you.

We are fortunate to have a loving God. When we ask for forgiveness, He has assured us that He will forgive us. God has the ability to forgive but He also does something that humans can not do —at least not intentionally. God forgives us of our sins and then He forgets. He assures us, "He has removed our sins as far away from us as the east is from the west." (Psalm 103:12, Living Bible). Micah 7: 19 states that,

"God will throw our sins into the depths of the ocean."

It's not as if God gets amnesia and forgets our sins, but he chooses to forget. Oh sure, he could remember if he wanted to, but he doesn't want to. Instead, he chooses to forget our confessed sins. We humans may try to forget but the more we try, the more we tend to remember.

God is a lot easier with us than we are with ourselves. He forgives and forgets. We tend not to forgive ourselves. In fact, have you ever asked for forgiveness for the same sin more than once - like two or three. . . or a hundred times? God has already forgiven us the first time we asked. The subsequent times we ask for forgiveness we are either trying to forgive ourselves or wanting to verify that God is actually forgiving us for something for which we cannot or will not forgive ourselves. Can you imagine God's reaction when we continually ask for forgiveness for something He has already forgiven and forgotten? I can imagine God saying, "What are you talking about?"

CHAPTER FOURTEEN

THE FIRST BIG ENDING

As I lie in bed surveying my room I again focus on my big screen TV. On the top are two VCRs, neither of which I have figured out how to use to record television programs. We use them for playing videos often. The one facing me is the most complicated. It is the newer model we got to go with the new TV. The other VCR is facing away from me. It is the one I bought about twelve years ago. As far as I am concerned, they just don't make them like that anymore. It plays and records. That's about it. The old one can be programmed to start and stop at a certain time much easier than the newer one.

The reason they are both sitting on top of my television at this time is because we have been copying some tapes from when I was recently on the news. Since I could not record the news, a friend recorded it for me and I have copied their tape.

A friend of mine recorded a presentation I gave at my church and I have since made several copies of it. This was my last big speaking engagement. Well, for some or maybe most people it may not have been that big of a deal but for me it certainly was.

On September 23, 1990, I spoke at a ladies luncheon at my church. I was honored to be the first member from our congregation to be asked to speak at this monthly luncheon. As I planned my talk, I had grandiose plans for perfecting this talk and speaking to other groups, like The Christian Women's Club of Fresno and The Christian Businessmen's Association. I even imagined someday teaming up with people like Joni Eareckson Tada and Billy Graham.

Later, I was talking to my friend Lorena about this. She cautioned me not to plan too far ahead. She reminded me that the Lord was in control and that we would have to wait to see what His plans were. What Lorena said caught me off guard. I had just assumed that God wanted me to share my message to glorify Him in this way. I did not understand what else He could have had in mind for me. I later realized that what the Lord had planned for me was very different from what I had planned.

The skeleton of this book came from my talk at this luncheon. I presented to them some of the information that is contained in this book; but I only talked for 30 minutes so there is much more here than I shared with that group. At the point I ended my talk, I wanted a big closing but my story was not and is not yet over.

LIFE GOES ON

My condition at the time I spoke was that I did not have use of my extremities. Although I had been in a wheelchair for over six years, my arms had only become dysfunctional during the previous year. The consequences of this that I had to have someone care for many of my needs. I could no longer feed myself, write, or drive my own van. This is when I lost a lot of my independence. I also stopped teaching disabled students at the local Community College. My pain and fatigue had increased to a point where I was not able to get to the college and still give the students the quality of teaching they needed. I miss them tremendously.

I shared with my audience what I was doing with my life at that time. I had a small counseling practice in my home. I was also doing some writing by dictating into a small recorder that my typist would transcribe. I had been writing articles, some of which had been published.

MY DOG/ MY CO-THERAPIST

One of the articles that I had in progress at the time of the luncheon talk was "My Dog the Therapist." This is about how my licensed service dog, Francine, helps me with my work. Francine, a beautiful golden retriever, and I are extremely close. Not only do my dog and I look alike with our strawberry-blonde hair, but we are alike in many other ways. We both adore my husband, we share some of the same interests, and we have some of the same skills. I studied for eight years to acquire these skills for therapy that she seemed to have naturally. In fact, at times I refer to her as my co-therapist.

I was very excited about graduating with my licensed service dog in February of 1988. Most of the dogs are presented to the disabled person by the individual who raised them as a puppy. No one could identify for me who had raised Francine. All things being considered, I just assume Francine is my special gift from God.

When I came home with Francine, she had a repertoire of eighty-nine commands to assist me in my wheelchair. She quickly learned even more commands. Francine could pick up items I had dropped, turn light switches on and off and even pull my wheelchair for me.

Francine and I go everywhere together. She especially likes church because she receives lots of attention from our friends. She really liked Sunday School when we taught first and second grade children. Sometimes I would ask a child to take care of Francine during the class. Actually, Francine would take care of the child. She would keep the noisy ones quiet and help the shy ones feel special.

Francine has a special way with people. She just seems to make them feel good. When I would counsel, Francine would go to her spot under my desk where she would lie down.

Occasionally, she would wander from her spot to help me with some clients by offering a hand to shake, head to pat or a look that said "I know you are hurting." Not only has Francine enriched my life, but she has also enriched the lives of many people that have come in contact with her.

HUGGING WHEELERS

My big project at the time of my luncheon talk was a manuscript called "How to Hug Someone in a Wheelchair." I had hopes that it would develop into a book. I feel, along with many other people, that hugging is very important. Hugging keeps us healthy. It helps to cure depression and reduce stress. Have you ever noticed that when you hug someone you may take a deep breath and sigh? This is a sign that tension is leaving your body. Hugging is nothing less than a miracle cure with no side effects. Ecclesiastes 3:5 says there is

"a time to hug and a time not to hug."
(Living Bible)

It is gratifying to know that there will be hugging in heaven, too. I definitely have plans to hug Jesus when I go home.
It is not really tricky to hug a person in a wheelchair. First of all, if they have a standard size wheelchair, I suggest placing a chair at their side so you are facing them. It is important to be at eye level if at all possible. This is the best position I have found to enjoy the hugging. If the wheelchair sits higher you must be a bit more creative. Try bending your knees or leaning over, whatever it takes for both of you to enjoy the hugging.
My writing project was constantly changing as my disability changed. When I lost the use of both of my arms, I

added a new chapter to the book entitled, "Look Ma, No Hands!" Without the use of arms, it is not easy to give and receive hugs. First of all, it is awkward because if I ask, "May I hug you?" - this is not accurate because I am not doing the actual hugging. But once the hugging starts people say I give great hugs. Yes, I mean even without using my arms. How, you may ask, do I accomplish this? I move my neck and have facial contact with the other person. In other words, I give great cheek hugs. As my disease has continued to progress my writing of "How to Hug Someone in a Wheelchair" has been put on hold. I have been called to do this priority project first.

CHAPTER FIFTEEN

AFTER THE LUNCH WAS OVER

As I lie in bed looking around my room I turn my eyes above my left shoulder where I see my control panel. This is what we named a group of controls for electronic devices around the house that we built in 1987. The idea was that I could have control over several aspects of the house from my bed. The top segment controls the security system. Apparently, this is an elaborate system, although I do not use much of it except to turn the alarm on and off.

The next segment of my control panel is the intercom. I find this to be very useful. It is connected to five other panels throughout the house and two outside panels. This makes it easier for my husband and, my assistants and me to find each other and to converse. Another feature on this segment is the door talk. This is a handy device to answer the door even from the back rooms of the house and also to screen the callers.

The third segment of my control panel consists of four switches. One operates my ceiling fan, which is usually left on all of the time. Another switch is for an outside light, which I just recently discovered. That leaves me with two additional switches; I have no idea what they control. My control panel leaves me with the illusion of control. But it is not my control. It is like everything else in the world. God has the control. Well, at least He has the plan. He gave us the freedom to choose whether to follow it or not. God had the control over what would become of my talk at the luncheon and the control over where I would go from there.

THE DAY AFTER

I was excited about expanding my presentation. I was contemplating with whom I might next share these experiences. I had heard of disabled people writing by using a pencil in their mouth. I thought that if I developed this skill I could expand my capabilities to work on my projects. I had one of my helpers attach a tongue depressor to a primary pencil. I held the tongue depressor in my mouth and wrote a total of eight words. It took a long time and the words were not neat, but at least they were legible. Then my jaw and neck started to get sore so I stopped to rest. As I rested the soreness worsened until my neck was in spasm. I could not speak more than a whisper for a couple of days and then it stopped. I had no voice at all.

I thought back to when I started to prepare my talk for the ladies luncheon. I remembered my friend Lorena had said to wait to see where the Lord would lead me. She was certainly right. My mission apparently was not to do the public speaking of my story like I had thought. God had other plans for me. My health, in general, deteriorated. I could not chew food and it was difficult for me to swallow. I had to learn to live on pureed food. I actually have not eaten lobster, which was my favorite, since the summer of 1990! I am looking forward to the feast in heaven since I am sure there will be lobster there.

DIRECTIONLESS

Eventually, I couldn't hold my head or shoulders up for very long, so I had to stay in bed most of the time. For six months, I would say I was seriously ill. I had no direction. I canceled my clients, but I had not given up on resuming my counseling practice.

In January, I had an MRI (Magnetic Resonance Imaging) test. This was a relatively new test which apparently can diagnose MS. It's a very expensive procedure performed with a very expensive machine. I was told that this was going to be uncomfortable and that I should take my medication before the test so that I could relax. The MRI involved lying on a table that moved into a cylinder. There were knocking sounds similar to a hammer. I was very relaxed and falling asleep. What I found annoying was the technician in the next room announcing when I was going to be hearing the knocking. If it were not for these interruptions I could have slept through the entire procedure.

Several months later I received the results in the form of seven pages of x-rays consisting of eighty-four pictures of my brain. I was not sure what all that meant and I am still not sure. At best I know I have a brain. If they could find that many views of which to take pictures, I must be smart, too.

DEALING WITH THE DIAGNOSIS

The doctors had several reasons for doing this test. First of all, they wanted to confirm the MS diagnosis for my records. They also wanted to see to what extent my other symptoms were related to the MS. When the results came back a nurse said jokingly, "Well, the tests say you have MS." I was devastated. I didn't remember the first time I was told I had MS. It wasn't significant to me then since I didn't know what MS was. Remember, I was only 20 years old at the time. Now I know only too well what this disease means.

With this retesting, I had an unrealistic hope that there would be another diagnosis, one that could be cured. Unfortunately, no such luck. With the confirmation of my diagnosis, I was again confronted with MS. This time, the diagnosis brought tears to my eyes. I tried to blink them away as I played the scenario in my mind. It was a scenario that I knew only too well, that of living with MS - a chronic illness. The MRI test also showed my other symptoms to be MS related. Considering my past history, the chances were that my voice and other functions that I had lost would not return. 1Thessalonians 5:18 says,

"Give thanks in all circumstances."

(NIV)

I was finding this very difficult to do at this point in my life. Still I held on to my faith in God.

I claimed and held fast to I Corinthians 10:13. This verse reads,

"No temptation has seized you except what is common to man. And God is faithful; he will not let you be tempted beyond what you can bear. But when you are tempted, he will also provide a way out so that you can stand up under it."

(NIV)

RELEARNING COMMUNICATION

As I mentioned before, my voice loss created a real difference in my relationships with others and especially with my husband. I also developed a deep depression. My futile attempts at communicating were frustrating, to say the least. In the past I had learned some sign language but now part of the alphabet was all my hands could maneuver.

About six months after my voice loss, I was introduced to an electrolarynx or voice amplifier. When this apparatus was held against my neck and a button was pressed, I was able to make audible words by moving my lips. Usually people who use such a machine are able to operate it by themselves. With the limited use of my hands I had to depend on someone else to help me talk. The important thing was that I was again able to communicate which changed my life drastically. Finally the change was for the better.

WHAT NOW?

I was still in bed most of the time, yet feeling a little bit stronger and thus less depressed. I was in more of a dealing mode and spending a lot of time in prayer with the Lord. Helpers came to take care of me and my house but still I was alone most of the time. During the time I spent in prayer with the Lord, I would ask, "What do I do now, what is your will for me?" Psalm 46:10 says,

"Be still and know that I am God."
(King James Version)

I had no alternative but to wait and listen.

THE ANSWER COMES

I had heard many times that anyone could be a missionary. I always responded sarcastically to myself, "Oh sure, how could I be a missionary in my condition? "One day I was listening to a tape of a sermon that my church had sent to me. One of the worship leaders spoke about how anyone could be a missionary. Then it struck me differently. I, too, could be a missionary even from my bed. I understood that there was another way for me to give my message to people besides the spoken word. With the help of some other people, I could do some writing.

The Lord and I were going to write a book. Now God had done this before; in fact, He wrote the world's best seller. I would have to depend on Him for guidance. I did not know what the title would be. I had my talk from the ladies luncheon and went from there.

There were a lot of mechanical things which we had to figure out. First of all, since I could not hold my electrolarynx myself, it was tiring for the person holding it. It was also tiring for me in that my neck got sore and I had to move my lips in such a distinct manner that my mouth got tired. Although my voice was audible, it took some getting used to since it was an artificial sound. In writing, one person had to hold my "voice" while another person did the actual writing. Since this was a tedious process, we could only work for short periods of time, maybe only an hour or so.

Of course, there are other factors in a project like this that must also be considered. So far the Lord has found the people to take care of these matters.

NEW DIRECTION

I now have a purpose and a goal in my life again. This gave me enough courage to officially close my counseling practice. I would like to say that chapter in my mind is closed, but I am afraid it never will be. I worked hard and it was such a difficult part of my life to give up that I will always have ties to it to some extent. Former clients still call and ask how I am, tell me how they are or ask if I will give them a referral. I listen to them on my speaker phone while one of my assistants relays my message. I must admit that I feel good that they still think of me as a person in whom they can confide. Although the number of calls that I receive from former clients has decreased in the years since I stopped counseling, there are a few who continue to call and even visit.

    Counseling had become such a big part of me that sometimes I have to hold back so as not to sound interfering when talking to these friends, and even with people in general. I have to keep reminding myself and sometimes them, that I no longer am their counselor. I guess now I am a writer and a missionary.

CHAPTER SIXTEEN

THE END FOR NOW

As I lie in my bed, directly above my head is a large wreath made of grapevines. The wreath is at least thirty inches across, faintly sprayed with a light pink paint and decorated with numerous flowers. When I went to have it made, I brought a piece of my wallpaper with me so the flowers could be matched according to kind and color. The silk flowers are predominantly mauve. Some people might call them pink, but I don't around my husband. He prefers having a mauve bedroom rather than a pink bedroom.

The flowers are arranged down the left side of the wreath in a half-moon fashion. My favorites are the white lilies in various stages of opening. They look almost like satin. I am glad we added the teal flowers. They bring out the teal in the entire wallpaper. I cannot identify any flower that looks like the teal ones, either in the wreath or wallpaper. Come to think of it, most of the mauve flowers don't resemble any real flower either.

Near the top right side of the wreath is a small arrangement of its own. It contains my favorite lily and the teal flowers. The mauve is brought out in a many-looped taffeta type ribbon. I find most wreaths like this one to be very pretty. I had a small part in designing it. Some other wreaths I do not find quite as attractive. Some remind me of the crown of thorns worn on the cross by our Savior, the Lord Jesus Christ. That unforgettable day, although painful to think about, is so important to our Christian faith. It is important to recognize that this was the beginning of the resurrection.

NOT YET

I would like to be able to say that my husband has accepted Jesus Christ as his Savior, but he is not ready to make that commitment yet. I know the day will come. I pray I will be here to see and be a part of our little Christian family.

Although it would not be accurate, I would like to be able to say that the Lord has chosen to completely heal me. That has not happened yet, but I know that too will occur, if not before, at least when I go home to be with Jesus.

PARTIAL HEALING

I have received some physical healing. February 1, 1993, I had a gastrostomy, a surgical procedure where a tube was inserted into my stomach. A couple of years before, my doctor had suggested that some day I would need a feeding tube. I shrugged that off immediately. I was doing just fine drinking pureed soups.

Later, my swallowing became more difficult as my MS progressed. I tried to drink nutritious canned drinks, but more was coming up than going down. Swallowing also became more painful. Anything that happened to make its way down my throat caused great agony. The medication I had been given to help me swallow was, in itself, difficult to swallow. It also made me very tired. Besides adding to my fatigue level, the clarity of my mind was being reduced.

Finally, I had become so weak that I decided, this is enough, and called a halt to everything. I had finally made the decision the doctor had predicted. It was time for me to get acquainted with a feeding tube.

No doubt I should have taken this step sooner. But, in retrospect, it's amazing to me that I had the ability to make the decision when I did, since my thinking had become so distorted with all the medication and lack of nutrition, I believe that God's timing was central to my decision to have a gastrostomy.

I certainly wasn't ready for the procedure earlier. It was crucial for me to experience the months of extreme discomfort in trying to swallow: that suffering time actually makes sense to me now. When people ask me, "Don't you miss eating?" or "doesn't it bother you to see other people eat?" I can honestly say no. This response is because, for a long time, I have associated swallowing, and therefore eating, with pain. If I had agreed to the gastrostomy earlier, and therefore not gone through that painful eating experience, I might be missing food. I could not have made the decision to have the tube inserted much later, since my nutrition would have been so bad by then that I would have probably continued to shrivel away.

So it looks as if the timing for this procedure was perfect, for which I cannot take credit. God was my pilot, rather than my copilot, at this point.

After the initial healing process from the surgery, my health continued to improve. My need for pain medication decreased and, of course, I didn't need the medications to help me swallow since I was consuming nothing by mouth. With less medication, my mind became clearer and my fine motor skills improved, therefore increasing my independence.

Tube feeding is not really that bad. In fact, it has some positive aspects. I don't have to worry about my weight or what I will have for my next meal. All I have to do is combine medication and canned nutrition. One particular advantage of tube feeding is that I can have my lunch and carry on a conversation at the same time!

CAN WE TALK?

I have also been blessed with a voice apparatus that I can operate by myself. The technicians at the bio-med unit at the Fresno Veterans Administration Hospital started with a Cooper-Rand voice amplifier. This unit was originally similar to the existing electrolarynx that I had been using. The difference in the new unit is that a plastic tube is placed in the mouth. The person holds the control unit in their hand and as they press a button and form words around the tube with their mouth, their voice becomes audible. Tom redesigned this apparatus so that I could use it. He attached a goose neck between the tube voice piece and a clamp that would attach to a table or my wheelchair. A wire runs from the mouthpiece to the control unit which I can attach anywhere with the miracle of Velcro. The lever to operate the unit is so sensitive it will respond to the slightest pressure. Now I am able to speak independently and even interrupt. I still use my original electrolarynx at times when I have writing teams helping me. This gives me a rest since different muscles are used with each apparatus.

THE LAST WORD

I was recently watching "Hour of Power," a television ministry presented by Dr. Robert Schuller from the Crystal Cathedral in Garden Grove, California. He told a story which I would like to share with you, along with my modified version.

This Chinese peasant man had one son. Their entire assets consisted of one horse. One day the horse ran away. The townspeople said, "What bad luck."

The Chinese peasant man, stroking his beard, responded, "How do you know it is bad luck?"

The horse returned home. Accompanying the horse were twelve wild horses. Neighbors came and exclaimed, "What good luck!"

Stroking his beard, the peasant man said, "How do you know it is good luck?"

One day the son was breaking a horse. After being thrown from the horse he suffered a broken leg. The son would be crippled for the rest of his life. The townspeople said, "Oh, what bad luck."

The peasant man responded, "How do you know it is bad luck?"

A warlord came and took all the able-bodied men to fight in a war. The only one left behind was the crippled son of the peasant. All of the men who had gone to war died. The townspeople responded, "What good luck."

The peasant man chuckled and without stroking his beard, said, "How do you know it is good luck?"

I would like to give an extremely modified version of this story as I see it relating to my MS.

"I have MS."
"What bad luck."
"How do you know it is bad luck? I came back to the Lord when I was in the hospital."
"Oh, what good luck."

Now this is where my story deviates from the story of the Chinese peasant. I can not say, like the Chinese peasant said, "How do you know it is good luck (to be with the Lord)?" I know from experience it is good to be with the Lord. We will have to go on from here, not questioning the desirability of being with the Lord, because it is good!

"When the Lord did not heal me like I requested, I became angry with God."
"Oh, what bad luck."
"How do you know it is bad luck?"
"When I got over my anger, my relationship with the Lord was much better."
"What good luck."
"Hallelujah!"
"Then my health became much worse."
"What bad luck."
"How do you know it is bad luck?"

I have become a missionary for the Lord and have rededicated my life to Jesus Christ. Let's all agree that this is good luck. I may be repeating myself, but this bears repeating. Romans 8:28 says,

"And we know that in all things God works for the good of those who love Him, who have been called according to his purpose."

(NIV)

The moral to all that I have been saying is that God will have the last word and it will be good.

MIRACLE?

In no way would I imply that MS is part of a miracle. But I know for a fact that my life has been 100% different than it would have been if I did not have MS.

I am not saying my MS is related to a miracle, but I do know I would not have come into contact with many of the wonderful people I have in my life if it were not for my illness. I am not suggesting that MS and a miracle could be related. But I received my education, established a productive family therapy practice and became a successful writer; accomphishments I don't think I would have attained under other circumstances. I have reached people through my counseling, speaking, teaching and writing that I may not have reached if I did not have MS.

I am not saying that MS is a miracle in my life. But God turns what we consider to be neagative situations into positive if we let Him. Remember, God performs miracles in the darndest ways.

WITH APPRECIATION

I would like to acknowledge the three spiritual leaders who have had a tremendous impact on my Christian life. I know God sent them to me or possibly sent me to them at crucial times. Although I have mentioned each of them at different times throughout this book, I would like to specifically acknowledge my gratitude for their influence.

Rev. Kirby Fuller was my first spiritual leader. He is the earliest memory I have of a minister in my life and was instrumental in providing me with a solid Christian background when I prepared to join the church. Not only was he our family's minister, but he and his wife Dixie were, and still are, good family friends. I even baby-sat their children.

My next spiritual leader was Chaplain Ron Climer, chaplain at the Fresno County Juvenile Hall. Although I really never knew Ron well, I consider him to be a good friend. It's hard to explain the bond I feel toward Ron. He was there with a listening ear when I needed it. For that I am forever grateful.

Dr. Alvern Vom Steeg—it's hard to know what to say about him. Yes, he was one of my spiritual leaders but he was more than that. He led me to a point where I could fly on my own. When he left Fresno and therefore St. Lukes United Methodist Church, I must admit I was nervous. I remain friends with Pastor Al and his wife Jane. Our correspondence and meetings are both too infrequent although I appreciate Jane maintaining this contact.

With Pastor Al's guidance, I had no need to worry. My relationship with Jesus Christ was strong. That's all I needed, that's all I will ever need.

THE MISSIONARY WRITING TEAM

For me, a project of this magnitude required a lot of help. Prayers and volunteer workers came from unimaginable places. We needed to do the usual proof reading, typing and the like. I also needed people to write as I dictated and, at times, to hold my artificial voice. Following are the names of miracle missionaries God sent to do the work:

Rita Alexander
Carol Amundson
John Baird
Lesli Barkema-Millard
Alvera Bauer
Shawn Becerra
Libby Beckstead
Richard Berrett
Karen Bowser
Jean Brewer
Chico Camerena
Dorothy Carr
Jean Chaffee
Connie Clendenan
Lourena Coker
Gail Connelly-Hamada
Denise Coté
Elain Crowder
Ruth Dawnson
Patti Dayton
Sarah Dayton
Stephanie Dayton
Jim Denney
Dee Ann Dominie

Giles Gillett
Melissa Green
Shari Hanlin
Bonnie Hearn
Carol Helander
Dana Johnson
Betty Kellems
Jacelyn Keller
Bobbye Kneeland
Jackie Little
Robin Little
Donna Lynch
Lisa Mabry
Robert Millard
Vic Montgomery
Judy Nesper
Freda Nettleton
Alma Nightengale
Don Norton
Brian Perez
Louise Petersen
Barbara Rosenthal
Patricia Rowe-Zeh
Tammy Schmidt

MIRACLES IN THE DARNDEST WAYS

Jacque French
Alvina Friederick
Aundrea Fry
Karen Fryer
Barbara Gillett

Doris Schwindt
Jennifer Schockey
Eric Silvius
Julia Tadich
Tad Tadich
Becky Williams

Thank you one and all!